PAUL DUNN

Single Quote Success: Simplify Selection, Ensure Excellence, Enjoy Peace of Mind

Why Getting 3 Quotes is a Waste of Your Time

Copyright © 2024 by Paul Dunn

©2024 Paul Dunn. All rights reserved.

No part of this publication may be reproduced, distributed, or transmitted in any form or by any means, including photocopying, recording, or other electronic or mechanical methods, without the prior written permission of the publisher, except in the case of brief quotations embodied in critical reviews and certain other noncommercial uses permitted by copyright law. For permission requests, write to the publisher at P. D. Electrical Services (SW) Ltd.

The information provided within this book is for general informational purposes only. While the author and publisher have worked to ensure the accuracy and completeness of the information conveyed in this publication, they make no representations or warranties of any kind, express or implied, about the completeness, accuracy, reliability, suitability, or availability with respect to the book or the information, products, services, or related graphics contained in the book for any purpose. Any reliance you place on such information is therefore strictly at your own risk.

In no event will the author or P. D. Electrical Services (SW) Ltd. be liable for any loss or damage including without limitation, indirect or consequential loss or damage, or any loss or damage whatsoever arising from loss of data or profits arising out of, or in connection with, the use of this book.

The author and publisher disclaim any financial responsibility for any kind of loss or risk incurred as a consequence, directly or indirectly, from the use and application of any contents of this book. Readers should consult professional advisors for advice on their particular circumstances.

First edition

This book was professionally typeset on Reedsy.
Find out more at reedsy.com

Contents

Introduction	1
THE MYTH OF MULTIPLE QUOTES: UNVEILING THE TRUTH	3
EFFICIENCY IN SINGLE-QUOTE STRATEGY	16
UNDERSTANDING SERVICE LEVELS AND EXPERTISE	29
COST ANALYSIS: PAYING FOR QUALITY, NOT JUST SERVICE	41
RISK MANAGEMENT IN CONTRACTING WORK	53
THE ART OF NEGOTIATION WITH A SINGLE CONTRACTOR	65
LEVERAGING TECHNOLOGY IN MODERN CONTRACTING	77
SUSTAINABLE PRACTICES AND YOUR ELECTRICAL NEEDS	90
THE PSYCHOLOGICAL BENEFITS OF SIMPLIFIED CHOICES	102
MASTERING THE SINGLE QUOTE APPROACH	114
SEIZE THE DAY: YOUR PATHWAY TO MASTERING CONTRACTOR CHOICE...	128
About the Author	131
Also by Paul Dunn	133

Introduction

Hi, I'm Paul Dunn, and I'm grateful you have chosen to read this book. With over 20 years of experience leading my own electrical services company, I've seen firsthand the confusion and frustration that many face when securing electrical services. The sheer number of choices, each contractor promising excellence but often falling short, can leave you overwhelmed and second-guessing your decisions.

Imagine embarking on a crucial project—whether it's revamping your home, upgrading your café, or expanding your business. Naturally, you want the best outcome, so you start gathering multiple quotes. But what if this well-intentioned practice is actually steering you away from success?

This book aims to simplify the process, ensuring you get the best without the stress. Instead of getting lost in the maze of multiple quotes, what if focusing on a single, carefully chosen quote could streamline your decision-making process and elevate the quality of your project's outcome? This approach isn't just hypothetical; it can lead to unparalleled success and peace of mind.

The complexity of obtaining reliable electrical work isn't just about finding someone skilled; it's about finding someone who aligns with your values, understands your specific needs, and can deliver without causing you stress or anxiety. The evolving technologies and regulations in the electrical industry only add to the stakes, making it harder to discern what's necessary and what's not.

By focusing on a single, outstanding contractor who aligns with your vision and values right from the start, you save time and build a relationship based on trust and mutual understanding. This isn't about cutting corners; it's about enhancing efficiency and ensuring that every minute and penny spent moves you closer to the outcome you desire.

Welcome to "Single Quote Success," where we challenge the conventional wisdom of "the more, the merrier" and guide you towards a simpler, more effective way to achieve excellence in every project you undertake. As you turn the pages, you will find the answers and insights you need to navigate these turbulent waters and secure a prosperous future in the industry. Here's to achieving success, one single quote at a time.

THE MYTH OF MULTIPLE QUOTES: UNVEILING THE TRUTH

"Too many choices can overwhelm us and cause us to not choose at all." – Sheena Iyengar

The Time-Consuming Nature of Gathering Multiple Quotes

Let's delve into a common scenario: you have a project, perhaps a renovation of your cosy living room, the refurbishment of your bustling office space, or maybe an upgrade to your quaint café's outdoor seating area. The first step, you've always been told, is to get multiple quotes. Sounds prudent, right? However, the time you think you're investing in making a wise decision could actually be leading you down a path of inefficiency and frustration. Here's the breakdown of why this seemingly logical step might not be quite as beneficial as it appears.

Identifying Reliable Contractors

Think about the last time you tried to find a contractor. Where did you start? A search online, a few calls to friends for recommendations, or perhaps a browse through local forums? The hunt for not just any contractor, but a reliable one, is akin to finding a needle in a haystack.

First off, there's the online research. You type in "best contractor near me" and are immediately bombarded with hundreds of options. Each contractor's website promises the best service and the highest quality, but as any seasoned homeowner or business owner knows, these promises are as variable as the British weather.

Then, you might try going through reviews. This in itself can be a full-time job. For each contractor that looks promising, you read through both the glowing and the ghastly reviews trying to discern who's the real deal. Reviews, while helpful, can often be polarised or, worse, outdated.

And let's not forget the recommendations from friends and family. While these can sometimes lead you to a gem, they're based on individual projects that may not necessarily align with your specific needs or expectations. What worked wonderfully for your neighbour's small bathroom renovation might not scale well to your complete kitchen overhaul.

The process is not just about checking a box. It's about ensuring that the person you're hiring can deliver your vision within your budget and timeframe. Each potential contractor needs to be evaluated, their previous work inspected, and their credentials verified. This isn't a quick phone call; it's hours of investigation, and with every additional quote, the hours stack up.

The Scheduling Conflicts

Having narrowed down your list to a few promising candidates, you now face the challenge of scheduling them to come and see your project. This step is crucial because a true estimate can't be given over the phone or via an email; it requires a physical walk-through.

Aligning your schedule with that of busy contractors is an exercise in patience and flexibility. Contractors are typically juggling multiple projects, and finding a slot that suits both parties can be as tricky as solving a Rubik's cube. It's not uncommon to have to book appointments weeks in advance, which directly delays your project's start date.

Once appointments are booked, they can often be rescheduled last minute as emergencies on other sites arise. Each reschedule adds to the delay and extends the period your project remains just an idea rather than a work in progress.

Delay in Project Commencement

This brings us to perhaps the most critical impact of gathering multiple quotes — the delay in your project's commencement. Each week spent waiting for another contractor to submit a quote is a week lost in the actual execution of the project.

For homeowners eager to improve their living space, or business owners looking to enhance their commercial premises, time is not just money; it's comfort and functionality too. The longer your project is on hold, the longer you are living in a construction-ready home or working around an inefficient space in your business.

Moreover, project timelines can be season-sensitive, particularly in the UK where weather can dictate construction schedules. A delay in getting started could mean missing the window of good weather, which then pushes your project into less favourable seasons, complicating the construction process further.

In conclusion, while the logic behind gathering multiple quotes is sound in theory — aiming to ensure competitive pricing and high-quality work — the practical implications often paint a different picture. The time invested in this phase can balloon, causing delays and frustrations that could have been mitigated by a more streamlined approach to selecting contractors. As we move forward, consider how this traditional wisdom measures up against modern-day project management efficiencies and whether there might be a better way to kickstart your next project.

The Confusion of Comparison

Varying Price Points Explained

When you dive into the process of obtaining quotes, one of the first hurdles you encounter is the seemingly inexplicable variation in price points. It's like walking into a market where every stall claims to sell the 'best' apples but at wildly different prices. Why does this happen?

Firstly, the cost of materials can fluctuate significantly between suppliers. Some contractors might use premium materials, which, while more costly, promise longer durability and better performance. Others might opt for more cost-effective solutions that don't compromise much on quality but are easier on your wallet.

Labour costs also play a pivotal role. More experienced professionals or those with specialised skills often charge a premium for their expertise. They justify this with faster turnaround times, more precise work, and potentially lower long-term costs due to reduced need for repairs or renovations.

Overheads can also vary widely. A larger business with more staff, a fancy showroom, and a fleet of branded vehicles has higher operating costs compared to a lean, home-based contractor. Each contractor includes these overheads in their pricing in different ways, which can make some quotes appear more expensive than others.

Understanding these variations is crucial, but it requires a good grasp of what exactly you're being offered. Without this, you're comparing apples to oranges rather than apples to apples, which brings us to the next layer of confusion: differences in service offerings.

Differences in Service Offerings

Imagine you're looking for someone to redesign your kitchen. One quote includes design, installation, and materials. Another quote seems cheaper but only covers installation. A third one offers design, installation, materials, plus a 10-year warranty. You're not just buying a service; you're buying a package, and each package offers different value.

Service scope can vary widely between contractors. Some might provide a comprehensive service which includes project management and obtaining necessary permits. Others assume you'll handle the administrative side yourself. Without a clear understanding of each service package's scope, you can't fairly assess which quote offers the best value.

Additionally, the level of customisation offered can affect the price. A bespoke service, tailored specifically to your needs and preferences, will naturally cost more than a standard, off-the-shelf solution. This customisation can be crucial, especially for complex projects that need to meet specific requirements or fit into unique spaces.

Navigating through these different offerings requires a sharp eye and a clear understanding of what's essential for your project. It's easy to get swayed by a low price, but the real question is what you're getting for that price. A cheaper quote that requires you to handle more aspects of the project yourself might end up costing you more in time and effort.

The Complexity of Technical Jargon

Now, even if you manage to understand the differences in pricing and service offerings, there's another layer of complexity: technical jargon. Every trade has its own language, and unless you're fluent in it, you can easily get lost.

Contractors might throw around terms like 'load-bearing walls', 'R-values', or 'circuit breakers'. Each of these terms packs a lot of meaning about the quality and safety of the work proposed. Not understanding these can lead to miscommunications and misjudgements about what's included and what's necessary.

Moreover, terms used to describe materials can also be baffling. What exactly is the difference between 'low-E glass' and 'tempered glass'? Knowing these terms can significantly impact your decisions, particularly regarding cost, efficiency, and durability.

The complexity increases when legal and regulatory jargon comes into play. Terms like 'code compliance', 'permits', and 'inspections' are not just formalities but essential aspects that can affect the timing and legality of your project. Misunderstandings here can lead to legal troubles or the need for costly corrections down the line.

Navigating this maze of technical language requires either a significant time investment in education or the assistance of a knowledgeable guide, typically an experienced contractor or consultant who can translate this jargon into plain English.

In conclusion, while gathering multiple quotes might seem like a prudent step, the variations in pricing, the differences in service offerings, and the maze of technical jargon all combine to make the comparison far from straightforward. This complexity not only makes the decision tougher but can also disguise the true value of what you're paying for, leading to choices that might not meet your needs or budget in the long term.

The Stress of Decision-Making

When you're standing at the crossroads of a decision, especially one that involves significant financial outlay or personal commitment, the weight of making the 'right' choice can feel overwhelming. This is particularly true in the realm of contracting work, where the stakes are high and the outcomes directly impact your daily life or business operations. In this part of our exploration into the myths of multiple quotes, we delve into the often under-discussed emotional and psychological toll that the decision-making process can take on you.

Analysis Paralysis

Imagine you're faced with several quotes, each presenting its unique blend of pros and cons, costs, and benefits. The more options you have, the harder it can seem to choose the best one. This isn't just a fleeting frustration; it's a cognitive burden known as analysis paralysis, where the fear of making the wrong decision leads to a cycle of overthinking and inaction.

You might find yourself obsessively comparing the minutiae of each quote, trying to forecast every possible outcome to avoid potential pitfalls. However, this often leads to an overload of information, making it increasingly difficult to make a decision at all. Each additional piece of data doesn't make the choice clearer; it just adds another layer of complexity.

The problem here is not the lack of information, but rather its abundance. In a world where we prize data and detailed analysis, it can be counterintuitive to realise that too much information can be just as crippling as too little. For you, as someone seeking to make an informed choice, the challenge isn't in gathering data but in sifting through it to find what's truly relevant. This is where simplifying your decision-making process can radically change your experience, shifting it from one of stress to one of confidence.

The Fear of Choosing Poorly

Closely tied to analysis paralysis is the fear of making the wrong choice. This is particularly poignant when the decision has significant financial implications or when your home or business's functionality is on the line. The fear isn't just about the financial outlay, though that alone can be daunting; it's also about the consequences of a choice that could lead to more hassle and expense down the line.

Consider this: you opt for the lowest quote, swayed by the immediate savings, only to find that the contractor has cut corners, leading to shoddy work that will need fixing sooner rather than later. Alternatively, you might choose the most expensive quote, equating high cost with high quality, only to discover that you've paid a premium for brand rather than for superior craftsmanship or materials. Each scenario breeds its own form of regret and self-reproach, feeding into the fear that next time, your decision might be just as flawed.

The key to navigating this fear isn't to seek perfection in your choice but to develop a robust method for evaluating your options. This involves prioritising what truly matters to you — be it budget, quality, or timing — and assessing how each quote aligns with those priorities. By simplifying your criteria, you reduce the fear associated with potential negative outcomes because your decision is grounded in your most valued aspects.

Emotional Toll of Indecision

The emotional impact of indecision is perhaps the most subtle yet pervasive effect of gathering multiple quotes. Each day spent wading through options, doubting your choices, and fearing the fallout of a decision can be emotionally draining. It's not uncommon to feel stuck, anxious, or even helpless in the face of such decisions. These feelings don't just cloud your judgment; they can also affect your wellbeing, leading to stress, sleeplessness, and a pervasive sense of unease.

Dealing with this emotional toll requires acknowledging that the stress you feel is both real and valid. It's not merely a byproduct of the process but a significant factor that deserves attention in its own right. Allowing yourself space to reflect on your emotional responses can be incredibly freeing. It helps you recognise that while some anxiety around big decisions is normal, it shouldn't dominate your decision-making process.

Moreover, stepping back to view the decision as part of a larger journey can alleviate some of the pressure. It's about seeing the choice not as a make-or-break moment but as one step in a longer path. This perspective can reduce the immediacy of the stress and help reframe the decision as a learning experience, regardless of the outcome.

In conclusion, while the quest for multiple quotes might seem like a thorough approach to decision-making, it's crucial to recognise the hidden costs involved — not just in terms of time and confusion but also in the emotional and psychological toll it can exact. By understanding these impacts, you can better navigate the complexities of decision-making, leading to choices that are not only wise but also conducive to peace of mind.

RECAP AND ACTION ITEMS

We've just demystified the common belief that obtaining multiple quotes is the most efficient way to ensure quality and value in any project, be it personal or professional. You've seen how the traditional approach can often lead to a significant drain on your time, create confusion, and even cause undue stress.

Now, let's translate these insights into actionable steps that you can implement today to streamline your decision-making process, save time, and reduce stress:

1. **Prioritise Quality Over Quantity**: Instead of reaching out to countless contractors, focus on finding one or two reputable providers. Use trusted sources, read reviews, and maybe even seek recommendations from friends or industry insiders. This approach saves time and increases the likelihood of quality outcomes.

2. **Simplify Your Evaluation Criteria**: Develop a clear set of criteria based on what's most important for your project—be it budget, timeframe, or specific expertise. This checklist will help you to quickly assess potential contractors without getting bogged down by the unnecessary details or technical jargon that often accompanies multiple quotes.

3. **Trust Your Gut**: Once you have all relevant information, trust your instincts. You've done the legwork, understood the varying offerings, and considered the financial aspects. Now, make your decision based on who you feel most comfortable with and who best meets your project's criteria.

4. **Set Clear Communication from the Start**: When you choose a contractor, set the tone for open and honest communication. Clearly express your expectations and be sure to discuss any potential concerns beforehand. This proactive approach will help in aligning both parties and can prevent misunderstandings down the line.

5. **Prepare for Flexibility**: Understand that no project goes

perfectly to plan. Prepare mentally for possible adjustments and maintain a flexible approach. This will help you to handle unexpected changes more efficiently and with less stress.

By focusing on these steps, you enhance your chances of a smoother, more satisfying project completion. Remember, the goal isn't just to get the job done; it's to get it done right with as little hassle as possible. Armed with a new perspective and practical strategies, you're now ready to tackle your next project with confidence and peace of mind.

EFFICIENCY IN SINGLE-QUOTE STRATEGY

"Time is the scarcest resource and unless it is managed, nothing else can be managed." – Peter Drucker

Streamlining Your Selection Process

Embarking on any project, whether as a homeowner or a business owner, often involves the critical step of selecting a contractor. The traditional advice of gathering multiple quotes feels reassuringly thorough but is surprisingly inefficient. Let's deep dive into a more streamlined, single-quote strategy that not only simplifies the selection process but also paves the way for better outcomes and peace of mind.

Criteria for Choosing a Contractor

First things first, how do you zero in on that one, perfect contractor without the safety net of multiple quotes? It starts with establishing a set of non-negotiable criteria tailored to your specific needs and the demands of the project.

Consider expertise and experience as primary criteria. A contractor who has a proven track record with projects similar to yours is invaluable. Look beyond the number of years in the industry; seek out specifics that align with your project. For instance, if you're renovating a historic home, a contractor experienced in modern apartment buildings might not be your best bet despite their years in the business.

Next, evaluate their resource availability. Does the contractor have a reliable team and access to the necessary materials and equipment? Delays in sourcing can significantly extend project timelines and inflate budgets.

Licensing and insurance should also be on your checklist. These not only verify professional credibility but also protect you from potential liabilities. Ensure the contractor holds all necessary local and national certifications and is insured to cover any mishaps during the project.

Lastly, consider their project management capabilities. How do they plan and communicate timelines? A contractor who provides a clear, detailed plan with built-in accountability measures is more likely to deliver on time and to specifications.

The Power of Referrals

In an age where information is just a click away, the age-old power of referrals remains undiminished. Referrals from trusted sources act as a pre-screening tool, significantly reducing the risks associated with hiring.

Start with your network. Reach out to friends, family, or business associates who have recently undertaken similar projects. They can provide insights not just on the work quality but also on the contractor's communication and problem-solving skills. A positive experience in your network can be a strong endorsement.

Additionally, tap into local trade associations or chambers of commerce. These organisations often have stringent criteria for membership, meaning a referred contractor through these channels likely meets a baseline of professional standards.

Remember, a referral goes beyond mere recommendation; it's an opportunity to ask detailed questions about the contractor's reliability, adaptability, and overall professionalism. Use these insights to gauge whether they align with your project's needs and your working style.

Online Reviews and Ratings

While personal referrals are golden, online reviews and ratings are indispensable tools for validating your choice. They provide a broader perspective, offering a blend of positive and negative experiences from a wide range of clients.

Start with reputable trade websites or platforms specific to the construction and renovation industry. Look for contractors who not only have high ratings but also a substantial number of reviews. A 5-star rating from three reviews might not be as convincing as a 4.7-star rating from fifty reviews.

Read beyond the stars. Detailed reviews can reveal specifics about a contractor's strengths and weaknesses. For instance, comments about professionalism, adherence to budget, and timeliness are critical. Also, pay attention to how contractors respond to reviews, particularly negative ones. This can be telling of their customer service orientation and willingness to resolve issues.

However, maintain a critical eye. Online reviews can be manipulated. Cross-reference by checking more than one source, and consider the overall trends rather than isolated comments.

By integrating these elements – a clear criteria list, leveraging the power of referrals, and validating through online reviews – you can confidently select a contractor without the need to juggle multiple quotes. This not only streamlines your selection process but also sets a solid foundation for the subsequent phases of your project. Remember, the goal here is not just to simplify but also to enhance the quality of your contractor engagement, ensuring a smoother project flow and ultimately, peace of mind.

Building Trust and Rapport

When you embark on a project, whether renovating your home or upgrading your business facilities, the relationship you forge with your contractor can significantly impact the outcome. It's about more than just getting the job done; it's about building a partnership based on trust and mutual respect. Let's explore how personal interactions, consistent communication, and the cultivation of long-term relationships can transform your single-quote strategy into a streamlined path to success.

Importance of Personal Interaction

First impressions matter. When you meet a contractor for the first time, think of it as more than just an assessment of their skills and a quote for your project. This is your opportunity to gauge their professionalism, their passion for the project, and their ability to connect on a human level. Personal interaction here is key. It's during these initial meetings that you get a sense of their honesty, integrity, and the respect they have for your vision.

Engage them in conversation. Discuss not only the specifics of the project but also their previous experiences and even challenges they've faced in similar projects. How they address your concerns and communicate their ideas can tell you a lot about how they will handle your project. It's crucial that they not only listen to your ideas but also understand your expectations. This mutual understanding is the foundation of trust.

Remember, the goal of these interactions should be to build a rapport that makes you comfortable enough to entrust them with your investment. You are not just hiring a service; you are partnering with a professional who will help realise your vision.

Consistency in Communication

Once the project kicks off, consistent communication becomes the thread that keeps the partnership strong. Regular updates from your contractor can remove a lot of the stress typically associated with such projects. It's reassuring to know the status of your project and being kept in the loop helps in building trust.

Set up a communication plan at the start. Decide how often you would like updates and through what means – be it emails, phone calls, or face-to-face meetings. Some prefer a weekly summary, while others might like more detailed daily updates. This not only keeps you informed but also gives you an opportunity to provide feedback, making you an active participant in the project.

It's also important for your contractor to communicate proactively. If unforeseen issues arise, as they often do, you should hear about them from your contractor first, along with proposed solutions. This level of transparency is crucial. It shows that they value your satisfaction and are committed to maintaining the integrity of your project.

Long-term Relationship Benefits

Thinking long-term might not be your first instinct when hiring a contractor, but establishing a relationship that extends beyond a single project can offer immense benefits. A contractor who has worked with you before will have a deep understanding of your preferences and how you operate. This can streamline future projects, as much of the initial groundwork of establishing trust and communication style has already been done.

Moreover, a lasting relationship can often mean preferential treatment. In busy periods, for instance, your contractor might prioritise your projects over new clients. They may also be more willing to negotiate costs and go the extra mile to meet your needs, knowing that maintaining a good relationship with you pays off long-term.

Additionally, a trusted contractor can become a valuable resource, offering advice and recommendations that go beyond just their contracted duties. They can alert you to potential maintenance issues before they become costly problems, or suggest improvements that increase the value of your property.

In building a long-term relationship, remember that loyalty goes both ways. Just as you benefit from their enhanced understanding and prioritisation of your projects, they benefit from steady work and the security of a reliable client. It's a partnership that fosters not just individual projects, but a collaborative growth over time.

Through effective personal interactions, consistent communication, and the cultivation of long-term relationships, building trust and rapport with your contractor can significantly elevate your project's success. This approach not only simplifies the selection process but enriches the journey, ensuring each project is handled with care and professionalism. By focusing on these elements, you create more than just a working relationship; you build a partnership that can last for years, simplifying future projects and ensuring peace of mind.

Time Saved is Sanity Gained

In the whirlwind world of project management, whether you're revamping your home or jazzing up your business space, time is not just a resource; it's the canvas on which efficiency and peace of mind paint their masterpieces. Embracing the single-quote strategy is akin to choosing the express lane, allowing you to bypass the often unnecessary congestion of multiple bids and dive straight into the good stuff—getting things done. Let's explore how this approach not only accelerates project kickoff but also reduces administrative overheads and frees up your schedule for more personalised project oversight.

Quicker Project Start

Imagine this: you've decided to renovate your kitchen. You're picturing sleek new countertops, state-of-the-art appliances, and cabinetry that perfectly aligns with your aesthetic. Now, you could spend weeks, even months, gathering and comparing quotes, or you could select a trusted contractor based on solid referrals and credible online reviews, and kick things off almost immediately. The single-quote strategy simplifies the initiation of any project by cutting down the prelude.

When you opt for multiple quotes, each additional quote adds not just another option to consider but also extends the timeline before any real work begins. It's not just about receiving the quotes; it's about analysing them, understanding the different scopes, and often going back and forth to negotiate terms. This can be especially cumbersome if the project is urgent or if you have a tight schedule.

Selecting a single, trusted contractor allows you to bypass these preliminary hurdles. With a clear choice, the focus shifts rapidly from planning to execution. You discuss, decide, and deploy—all in a timeframe that multiple quotes can seldom match. This efficiency is crucial not just for time-sensitive projects but also for reducing the mental load that prolonged decision-making processes invariably bring.

Less Administrative Hassle

Let's face it, dealing with paperwork and managing communications can be as draining as the physical aspects of a project. Each contractor interaction involves a trail of emails, phone calls, and meetings, not to mention the contractual paperwork that each party brings to the table. Now multiply this by three or more if you're juggling multiple quotes. It's not just about the physical time spent; it's the cognitive load of keeping track of each conversation, each promise, and each condition.

When you streamline the process to a single quote, you cut through this red tape dramatically. You have one set of documents to review, one set of terms to negotiate, and one point of contact. This streamlined communication not only saves time but also reduces the chances of misunderstandings and errors that can often arise from juggling multiple contractors.

Moreover, this approach allows for a more organised project management process. With fewer parties in the mix, scheduling becomes more straightforward, and there's a clear line of accountability. This simplicity in administration not only speeds up the project timeline but also provides a more transparent overview of the entire project, which is often appreciated in both residential and commercial settings.

More Time for Personal Oversight

With the foundations laid quickly and less clutter in the administrative process, what you're left with is what every project manager or homeowner yearns for—more time. This isn't just any time; it's quality time that can be spent on overseeing the finer details of your project, ensuring that everything is aligning with your vision.

In traditional multi-quote scenarios, much of your energy is expended in the selection phase, leaving you drained by the time the real work begins. However, with a single-quote approach, your energy reserves are preserved for the project execution phase. You can be more present on-site, engage more deeply with your contractor, and make timely decisions that keep the project flowing smoothly without delays.

This active involvement not only enhances the quality of the outcome but also ensures that the project truly reflects your personal or brand identity. It's an opportunity to infuse your space with your essence, without the distraction of ongoing negotiations or administrative chaos.

In conclusion, while the concept of gathering multiple quotes has its merits in certain contexts, the single-quote strategy offers a compelling alternative for those looking to minimise preliminary delays, reduce administrative burden, and maximise personal engagement in the project. By choosing this path, you're not just opting for simplicity; you're choosing a strategy that respects your time and sanity, ensuring that your project doesn't just meet your expectations but is an enjoyable journey from start to finish.

RECAP AND ACTION ITEMS

Congratulations! You've just navigated through the core principles of the Single-Quote Strategy, a method designed to streamline your decision-making process, build meaningful relationships with contractors, and reclaim valuable time. Now, let's put this strategy into action.

First, refine your selection criteria. Identify what truly matters to you in a project – be it the budget, the timeline, the materials used, or the contractor's expertise. Write these down. Remember, clarity here is crucial. The clearer you are, the easier it will be to communicate your vision and vet your contractor based on these outlined priorities.

Next, leverage the power of referrals and online reviews. Reach out to friends, family, and trusted colleagues who have undertaken similar projects. Their insights can provide you with invaluable, real-world perspectives on potential contractors. Complement this by researching online reviews and ratings. Look for patterns in feedback that align with your priorities. This dual approach will help you feel more confident in your choice.

Then, focus on building trust and rapport. When you meet with your potential contractor, engage in open and honest communication. Express your needs clearly and listen attentively to their responses. Consistent communication is key – it prevents misunderstandings and builds a foundation of trust. Remember, this could be the beginning of a long-term relationship that might benefit future projects.

Finally, appreciate the time you've saved. By adopting the Single-Quote Strategy, you can avoid the often exhaustive and confusing process of juggling multiple quotes. This streamlined approach not only accelerates the project's commencement but also reduces administrative burdens, freeing you up to focus more on overseeing the project or spending time on other important activities.

Your action plan is straightforward:

1. Define your project criteria

2. Gather referrals and check online testimonials

3. Engage personally and communicate consistently with your chosen contractor

4. Start your project sooner and oversee it with more personal attention.

By implementing these steps, you will simplify the selection process, ensure excellence in your undertakings, and enjoy peace of mind knowing you've made a well-informed decision.

Here's to making your next project a resounding success with minimal fuss and maximum satisfaction.

UNDERSTANDING SERVICE LEVELS AND EXPERTISE

"Quality is never an accident; it is always the result of intelligent effort." - John Ruskin

Decoding Industry Standards

When you're delving into the world of hiring professionals, whether it's for revamping your home or upgrading your business infrastructure, understanding the maze of industry standards can be as crucial as choosing the right colour for your living room walls or the perfect location for your new office. Let's break down these standards into three digestible parts: certifications and qualifications, industry accreditations, and continuing professional development. Grasping these elements will gear you towards making informed decisions, ensuring you engage with true professionals who bring both skill and integrity to your projects.

Certifications and Qualifications

First off, let's talk about certifications and qualifications. Imagine you're at a bustling market, each stall loudly advertising the 'best' fruit. How do you pick? You'd probably look for signs that indicate quality, such as organic certification or a farmer's mark, right? In the professional services world, certifications and qualifications play a similar role.

For trades like electrical contracting, plumbing, or building, specific certifications can tell you a lot about the practitioner's ability to meet industry standards and comply with local regulations. For instance, an electrician might be certified by the City & Guilds, which offers courses and qualifications on electrical systems, installations, and the latest wiring regulations. These aren't just fancy pieces of paper; they are rigorous assessments that professionals undergo to prove their competence and safety knowledge.

Why does this matter to you? Well, hiring someone with the right certifications means that the work done will not only be up to standard but will also comply with the latest health and safety regulations, reducing the risk of accidents or failures. It's about ensuring that the person handling your electrical wiring isn't just going by gut feeling but following well-established industry practices.

Industry Accreditations

Moving on to industry accreditations, these are somewhat like the Michelin stars of the service world. They provide an at-a-glance assurance that the professional you're considering has been recognised by industry bodies for their expertise and reliability. Accreditations are typically awarded by professional associations and institutions that represent a particular industry. They assess a range of criteria, including the quality of work, customer service, and ethical standards.

For example, in the building industry, you might look for a contractor who is a member of the Federation of Master Builders (FMB). This accreditation is a signal to you, the customer, that the contractor has met stringent standards and is committed to upholding quality craftsmanship. It's like a shorthand that saves you from having to dig into the minutiae of a contractor's work history; a seal of approval that tells you they've been vetted and approved by their own industry peers.

Continuing Professional Development

Lastly, let's consider continuing professional development, or CPD. This is where professionals continue to learn and update their skills throughout their careers. Why should you care? Because industries evolve, technologies advance, and regulations change. A professional who engages in CPD is someone who stays on the cutting edge, continually enhancing their skills and knowledge. It's a good indicator that they're not just resting on their laurels but are committed to providing the best and most up-to-date service possible.

In practical terms, this could mean an IT professional who takes courses in the latest cybersecurity practices to better protect your business data or a builder who attends seminars on sustainable materials and eco-friendly building techniques. By choosing professionals who prioritise CPD, you're opting for those who are not only qualified and accredited but who are also innovating and adapting in their fields. This aspect of professional growth ensures that the service you receive isn't just adequate—it's cutting-edge.

Recognising the importance of certifications, accreditations, and CPD will significantly streamline your search and hiring process. It allows you to quickly identify who meets the high standards you require for your projects and to sift through the myriad options with confidence. By understanding these industry standards, you're more equipped to select professionals who not only bring the requisite expertise and qualifications but who also demonstrate a commitment to maintaining high standards in their work and ongoing professional development. This knowledge arms you with the ability to make choices that align with both your immediate needs and your long-term satisfaction.

Assessing Technical Expertise

Essential Skills for Electrical Contractors

When you're on the hunt for an electrical contractor, knowing what technical skills are essential can be your golden ticket to ensuring you're not just getting a good deal, but also a safe and high-quality service. Electrical work is intricate and demands a high level of precision and knowledge.

Firstly, troubleshooting skills are non-negotiable. A top-notch electrician should be able to quickly identify problems and offer effective solutions. This requires a deep understanding of electrical systems and the ability to think logically and creatively under pressure. Whether it's a flickering light or a major power outage, you want someone who can diagnose the issue swiftly and efficiently.

Next up is the ability to read and understand complex blueprints and technical diagrams. These documents are the roadmap of all the electrical systems in a building. They show how these systems interact and detail the location of panels, circuits, and outlets. If your contractor can't navigate these blueprints, they're essentially flying blind.

Installation skills are also crucial. This is the bread and butter of any electrical contractor's skill set. It involves not only laying out and connecting wires but also ensuring that they comply with all safety standards and regulations. The way your contractor handles the installation can significantly affect the safety and efficiency of your electrical system.

Finally, a thorough knowledge of safety codes and regulations is essential. Electrical work can be hazardous, and compliance with national and local safety standards is not optional. An adept electrician should be up-to-date with the latest safety protocols and able to apply them to every project, ensuring a safe environment for all occupants of the building.

Innovations in Electrical Contracting

Staying abreast of the latest technological advancements can significantly enhance the service quality of electrical contractors. Innovations in the field are not just about using the newest tools, but also about adopting new methodologies that improve efficiency and safety.

One of the game changers has been the integration of smart technology into electrical systems. Smart tech allows for the remote monitoring and control of electrical systems, which can help in energy management and significantly reduce costs. For instance, smart thermostats and lighting systems can learn your habits and adjust themselves to save energy without your input. When seeking out electrical contractors, consider those who are knowledgeable about these technologies and can offer you solutions that integrate them.

Another innovation is the use of augmented reality (AR) in electrical contracting. AR can help electricians visualize electrical systems through a device, providing a layer of digital information that can guide repairs and installations without the need to open up walls or disrupt your space. This can lead to faster repairs and less invasive installations.

Moreover, the adoption of green technologies and practices is increasingly important. If sustainability is a priority for you, look for contractors who are skilled in installing solar panels, energy-efficient lighting, and other green systems. These technologies not only help reduce your carbon footprint but can also be economically beneficial in the long run.

Practical vs Theoretical Knowledge

While theoretical knowledge is undoubtedly important, in the world of electrical contracting, practical knowledge weighs just as heavily. This is the knowledge that electricians gain through hands-on experience, which is critical to mastering the craft.

Practical knowledge enables an electrician to apply learned theories to real-world scenarios. It's the difference between knowing what a circuit breaker does and being able to determine why a breaker keeps tripping and fixing it correctly. Practical experience also builds problem-solving skills that are crucial when unexpected issues arise during a job.

However, this doesn't mean you should discount the importance of formal education and theoretical understanding. A solid grasp of electrical theory is essential for understanding why systems work the way they do and ensuring that work is performed correctly the first time. The ideal contractor should have a balance of both: the theoretical grounding to understand the complexities of electrical systems and the practical expertise to implement solutions effectively.

When evaluating potential contractors, consider their educational background as well as their practical experience. Those who have apprenticeships or have worked under experienced mentors will have had the opportunity to develop a robust practical skill set. Also, check if they pursue continuing professional development to enhance their knowledge and keep up with the latest electrical practices and technologies.

In sum, when you're looking to hire an electrical contractor, delving into their technical expertise can make all the difference. Ensure they not only have the necessary skills and are up-to-speed with the latest innovations but also balance their theoretical knowledge with ample practical experience. This approach will help you choose a contractor who can deliver not just what you need, but also what you envision, safely and efficiently.

Recognising Quality and Craftsmanship

Workmanship Guarantees

When you're diving into the world of selecting a service provider, one of the first things you should eye is the workmanship guarantee. This isn't just about ensuring that someone comes back to fix things if they go belly-up; it's about setting the tone for the entire relationship. A robust guarantee signals that the contractor stands squarely behind their work, which in turn speaks volumes about their confidence in their skills and dedication to quality.

Imagine you're choosing a contractor for a significant home renovation project. Those who offer comprehensive workmanship guarantees are effectively telling you, "We do it right the first time." But what does a good guarantee look like? Typically, it should cover all aspects of the workmanship for a period that gives you ample time to live with and evaluate the work under various conditions.

The length and breadth of these guarantees can vary, but a one-year guarantee is a common standard. This should cover you for all seasons, allowing you to observe how the work holds up under different weather conditions, which is particularly crucial for exterior work. However, some top-notch providers might offer guarantees extending up to five years, a testament to their superior materials and techniques.

Moreover, the clarity with which a company communicates its guarantee often reflects their service quality. A transparent, easy-to-understand guarantee without a barrage of legal jargon can ease your mind and indicate a straightforward, customer-focused approach.

Quality of Materials Used

Moving beyond the promises of solid workmanship, the calibre of materials used can either be a silent endorsement or a secret detractor of the overall quality. The truth is, even the most skilled artisan can't produce first-rate work if the materials at hand are subpar. Therefore, understanding the quality of the materials involved in your project is crucial.

For example, in a roofing project, materials range from standard asphalt shingles to high-end slate or tiles. The difference in longevity, appearance, and performance between these options is vast. While it might be tempting to opt for cheaper materials to cut costs, this can lead to increased maintenance or even a full replacement much sooner than anticipated.

When discussing materials with potential contractors, ask

them to explain why they opt for certain brands or types. Trusted contractors will be able to provide detailed information about the advantages of higher-quality materials and how they contribute to the longevity and aesthetics of the work. Some might even offer options at different price points, explaining the lifecycle costs associated with each.

Past Project Reviews

Last but not least, the litmus test of all claims to quality and craftsmanship lies in what previous clients have to say. Past project reviews are gold dust for gauging the real-world application of a contractor's skills and the durability of their completed projects.

In today's digital age, accessing reviews has never been easier. Platforms like Trustpilot, Google Reviews, and specialized trade sites provide a plethora of client feedback at your fingertips. However, while online reviews are handy, they should be approached with discernment. Look for reviews that are detailed and project-specific, as they often give more insight than generic praise.

For an even better assessment, ask the contractor for case studies or the contact details of previous clients. Reputable service providers will be proud to showcase their work and connect you with past clients. This direct feedback loop can provide peace of mind and also give you a glimpse of the contractor's client service approach.

Visiting completed projects, if possible, offers an invaluable perspective. It allows you to see firsthand the ageing of materials, how well the craftsmanship has held up, and whether the work truly lives up to the promises.

By thoroughly examining these three crucial elements – workmanship guarantees, quality of materials, and past project reviews – you'll equip yourself with a comprehensive understanding of what true quality and craftsmanship entail. This knowledge not only aids in making an informed choice but also sets the stage for satisfaction and peace of mind in your project outcomes. Remember, in the realm of service selection, thoroughness is not just about diligence – it's about securing value that stands the test of time.

RECAP AND ACTION ITEMS

Now that you've delved into the intricacies of service levels and expertise, you're equipped with a robust framework to discern the qualifications, technical acumen, and craftsmanship of potential service providers. Whether you're a homeowner or a business owner, understanding these aspects ensures you're making an informed decision, not just collecting arbitrary quotes.

Firstly, reflect on the certifications, accreditations, and ongoing professional development of the providers you're considering. These elements are not just fancy titles but are pivotal in establishing the credibility and up-to-date knowledge of a contractor. Action Step: Create a checklist of essential certifications relevant to your needs and verify these credentials with potential contractors during your initial interaction.

Secondly, assess the technical expertise. The balance between practical and theoretical knowledge is crucial, especially in fields requiring technical precision like electrical contracting. Innovations in the industry can significantly affect service quality and efficiency, so prioritising contractors who demonstrate a commitment to using cutting-edge techniques can be beneficial. Action Step: Ask potential contractors to provide examples of how they've integrated new technologies or methods into their work and gauge their ability to explain these advancements clearly and concisely.

Finally, the quality of materials and workmanship guarantees are telltale indicators of a contractor's commitment to quality and reliability. Reviewing past projects and soliciting feedback from former clients can provide insights into the consistency and durability of a contractor's work. Action Step: Request references and conduct site visits to past projects if possible. Additionally, ensure that any guarantees or warranties offered are in written form and cover a satisfactory duration.

By taking these steps, you position yourself not just as a passive quote collector, but as a proactive, informed client who values quality and expertise. This approach will not only save you time and resources but also grant you peace of mind knowing you've entrusted your project to the best possible hands. Remember, the cheapest quote isn't always the best—but the best-informed choice usually is.

COST ANALYSIS: PAYING FOR QUALITY, NOT JUST SERVICE

"The bitterness of poor quality remains long after the sweetness of low price is forgotten." – Benjamin Franklin

The Real Cost of Bargain Hunting

In an era where every penny counts and budgeting becomes almost a form of modern art, the allure of bargain hunting can be irresistible. After all, who wouldn't want to save a bit of cash when dealing with renovations, repairs, or building services? However, the cheapest option isn't always synonymous with the best value. Let's delve into the hidden depths of opting for the lowest bid and uncover the real costs that might not be apparent at first glance.

Long-term Costs of Cheap Work

Imagine this: you choose the lowest quote for a house painting job. It looks fine, at least for a few months. Then, the paint starts to chip, the damp starts to seep through, and suddenly you're faced with a redo. Not only have you paid once, but now you're paying for the same job twice, potentially more if the underlying issues have worsened.

Cheap work often means corners have been cut. Whether it's inadequate surface preparation, inferior paint, or rushed labour, the initial savings can quickly turn into a financial sinkhole. The long-term costs aren't just monetary; consider the time spent dealing with follow-up repairs and the stress that comes with it. Plus, frequent replacements or repairs increase your carbon footprint, an environmental cost we can all do without.

Risks of Under-Qualified Contractors

When a quote comes in suspiciously low, it's a red flag that the contractor may be under-qualified. The building and renovation industry relies heavily on skilled labour, and true expertise comes at a price. Under-qualified contractors might not be up-to-date with building codes or may use improper techniques that could lead to significant issues down the line.

For instance, electrical work done poorly isn't just a minor inconvenience—it's a serious safety hazard. From increased risk of fire to the potential for electrical failure, the stakes are exceptionally high. The same goes for plumbing. A mistake in this area can lead to leaks, water damage, and costly water bills, not to mention the potential health risks from mould and mildew.

Choosing an under-qualified contractor can also affect your property's value. If you decide to sell your home or business space, savvy buyers will scrutinise the quality of the work done. Subpar work can dramatically decrease your property's market value, making that initial low-cost option even more expensive in the long run.

Hidden Costs in Low Bids

Low bids might seem attractive on paper, but they often exclude essential elements that are only discovered during the job. This is a classic case of bait and switch, where the final cost ends up being much higher than initially quoted.

Material costs are a common area where expenses can be hidden. A contractor might quote low, planning to use inferior materials that won't last or perform as well as you'd expect. Suddenly, you're faced with additional costs for upgrading materials mid-project, which not only disrupts your timeline but also your budget.

Then there's the issue of "extras." Some contractors provide a low initial quote but then charge extra for every little adjustment or unforeseen issue that inevitably arises. These additional charges can quickly tally up, leaving you with a final bill that bears little resemblance to the original quote.

Moreover, consider the time cost. Delays are common when contractors are juggling multiple projects, especially if they've made low bids to win several contracts. Each delay in your project means more time when your home or business isn't functioning as it should, which can translate to lost revenue or personal upheaval.

Bargain hunting, when it comes to contracting work, can indeed seem like a sensible move from a financial standpoint. However, as you peel back the layers of initial savings, the spectrum of potential costs and risks begin to surface—costs that are not just financial but also emotional and practical. Choosing a contractor should be about balancing cost with quality, credentials, and reliability. Remember, paying a bit more upfront can often save a lot of money, time, and stress in the long run.

Value Over Price

Investing in skilled labour, the use of high-quality materials, and the adoption of modern techniques might initially appear as a hefty expenditure. However, when you peel back the layers, you'll find that this approach isn't just about spending more; it's about investing wisely to save more in the long run. Let's delve into why prioritising value over price can lead to significantly better outcomes for your projects, whether you're sprucing up your home or giving your business a facelift.

Investing in Skilled Labour

You might have come across offers that seem too good to turn down — incredibly low rates with promises of quick completion. It's tempting, right? Here's the catch: the intricate dance of construction or renovation is best performed by those who have mastered the steps through rigorous training and years of experience. Skilled labourers bring precision, efficiency, and an ingrained understanding of the nuances of their craft.

When you choose skilled labour, you're not just paying for the hours they spend on your project; you're paying for the years they spent perfecting their skills. This translates to work that not only looks better but lasts longer. Skilled workers know how to avoid the common pitfalls that might not be apparent to the untrained eye. They can foresee potential problems before they become expensive fixes, and they can provide solutions that are both creative and effective.

Moreover, skilled workers are typically up-to-date with local building codes and regulations, which means you won't be facing compliance issues that could stall your project or lead to fines. Investing in skilled labour might cost more upfront, but it reduces the risk of costly errors and delays, ensuring that your project progresses smoothly and finishes on a high note.

Benefits of High-Quality Materials

Opting for cheaper materials can be one of the most tempting ways to cut costs. However, this is often a classic example of false economy. High-quality materials might dent your wallet more at the outset, but their longevity, durability, and aesthetic superiority can offer savings that lower-grade materials simply can't match.

Let's take the example of roofing materials. Cheap shingles might save you some pounds now, but they're also more likely to crack, leak, and blow off during storms. On the other hand, investing in high-quality slate or tiles might seem expensive, but these materials can last for decades, offering better insulation and requiring fewer repairs. This not only saves you money on maintenance but also on energy bills.

High-quality materials often come with better manufacturer warranties, giving you peace of mind and protecting your investment. They also tend to be more eco-friendly, reducing your environmental footprint and potentially qualifying you for green rebates or reductions in your insurance premiums.

Cost-effectiveness of Modern Techniques

Embracing modern techniques and technologies can be a game-changer. These methods are not just about following the latest trends; they are about making use of advancements that offer significant cost-effectiveness over traditional methods.

Take, for instance, the use of prefabricated components in construction. This technique allows parts of your project to be made in a controlled factory environment, which reduces waste and speeds up the construction process. The faster your project is completed, the less you spend on labour costs and the sooner you can enjoy or utilise the space, potentially generating revenue quicker if it's a commercial property.

Modern techniques like 3D printing in construction are also on the rise, allowing for precise and efficient material usage and labour allocation. Smart home technology is another area where modern advancements can save you money in the long term. Installing smart thermostats, lighting, and security systems can seem like a luxury, but they're actually investments that pay off through increased energy efficiency and enhanced security.

In summary, while it can be tempting to go for the lowest quote when planning a project, understanding the long-term financial benefits of investing in skilled labour, high-quality materials, and modern techniques can lead you to make decisions that will save you money and headaches in the future. Remember, when you choose value over price, you're not just buying a service or a product; you're investing in peace of mind and ensuring that your project stands the test of time.

Budgeting Smartly

Planning for Unforeseen Expenses

Let's kick things off with a truth bomb: the unexpected is not just a possibility when undertaking projects or renovations, it's almost a given. Whether you're refurbishing your home or overhauling your business premises, encountering unforeseen issues is part of the journey. What's crucial is having a buffer in your budget to manage these surprises effectively without causing a financial meltdown.

So, how do you plan for these unforeseen expenses? First, understand that no amount of planning can predict every hiccup. However, adding a contingency fund to your budget can be a game-changer. A good rule of thumb is to set aside 10-20% of your total budget. This might seem like a hefty addition, but it's preferable to the alternative of scrambling to find extra funds mid-project, which can be both stressful and more costly in the long run.

Think about potential hidden issues like electrical problems, plumbing surprises, or structural complications that often lurk unseen until work begins. By earmarking funds for unexpected costs, you're not just preparing financially, you're also cushioning yourself against the stress and potential delays these issues can cause.

Allocating Funds Wisely

Allocating your budget wisely is akin to balancing a scale. Lean too heavily on one side and the whole project might tip into disarray. It's essential to distribute your resources in a manner that maximises value without compromising on quality.

Start by prioritising the must-haves of your project. What are the non-negotiable elements that will ensure the safety, functionality, and aesthetics of your project? Once you've locked these down, you can consider how to allocate the remainder of your budget.

For instance, if you're renovating a kitchen, investing in high-quality appliances might take precedence over luxury finishes. Quality appliances not only last longer but also offer better energy efficiency, which can save you money in the long run. On the other hand, you might decide that bespoke cabinets, while nice to have, can be substituted with off-the-shelf products that are well-made but more cost-effective.

This approach isn't just about cutting costs; it's about making strategic decisions that align with your long-term goals and values. It's choosing to invest where it matters most to you and finding smart savings elsewhere. Remember, a well-planned budget is a flexible one, allowing adjustments as the project evolves while keeping the overall vision intact.

When to Splurge vs When to Save

Navigating the delicate balance between splurging and saving is more art than science. It requires a keen understanding of value—not just in terms of money, but also in terms of satisfaction and return on investment. Knowing when to open your wallet wide and when to snap it shut can make all the difference in achieving a blend of functionality and flair without overspending.

Splurging makes sense when the investment enhances the core value or utility of the project. For example, spending more on a high-efficiency boiler or a more durable roofing material makes sense. These are not just purchases; they're investments in the longevity and efficiency of your property. They reduce the need for replacements and repairs, and they can significantly increase your property's value if you decide to sell in the future.

Conversely, saving is wise when the items in question are either purely aesthetic or likely to be updated frequently. Paint colours, light fixtures, and decor elements, for example, can be areas where you can opt for less expensive options without compromising the overall quality of the project. Trends change, and it's likely you'll want to update these elements in a few years anyway.

Moreover, consider the lifespan and usage of the items. High-traffic areas might justify splurging on more durable flooring, whereas a guest bedroom might not necessitate top-of-the-line carpeting. The key here is to match the investment to the usage to ensure you're not overspending on underutilised areas.

In summary, smart budgeting isn't just about how much you spend, but how effectively you use your funds. It's about making educated choices that align with both your immediate needs and your long-term objectives. Whether you're splurging on essential items or saving on cosmetic changes, each decision should reflect your priorities and contribute towards a successful and satisfying completion of your project.

RECAP AND ACTION ITEMS

You've journeyed through an enlightening exploration of the hidden depths behind cost analysis, revealing that true value in services extends far beyond the initial price tag. You now understand that hunting for bargains can lead to a cascade of long-term expenses, under-qualified contractors pose significant risks, and that enticing low bids often mask unforeseen costs. Equally, you've seen the brighter side of investing in skilled labour, the undeniable benefits of choosing high-quality materials, and the cost-effectiveness that modern techniques bring to the table.

What's next, then? It's time to pivot this newfound knowledge into actionable steps to ensure that your next project—be it home improvements, business expansion, or anything in between—is both stress-free and successful.

1. **Evaluate the Total Cost of Ownership**: Before you sign any contracts, take a moment to consider the long-term implications of your choice. Cheapest isn't always best. Aim to understand the full lifespan cost of the services you are engaging. This might mean spending more upfront to save on future repair or replacement costs.

2. **Scrutinise Contractor Qualifications**: Always verify the credentials and past work of any contractor you consider hiring. Do they have a solid track record? Are there testimonials or reviews you can check? Make sure they are as good as they claim to be to avoid any costly mishaps down the line.

3. **Budget for the Unexpected**: As you plan your budget, allocate an additional 10-20% for unforeseen expenses. This safety net will help you manage any surprises without derailing your financial planning.

4. **Choose Quality over Cost**: When it comes to materials and techniques, opt for the best your budget can afford. Remember, high-quality choices often lead to reduced maintenance and longer intervals before replacement.

5. **Smart Saving vs Wise Splurging**: Be strategic about where to cut costs and where to invest more. Sometimes, spending a bit extra on a critical part of your project can save you money in the long run.

By integrating these steps into your approach, you'll not only ensure that you're paying for quality but also that you are setting yourself up for long-term satisfaction and peace of mind.

Remember, good decisions today will lead to fewer headaches tomorrow. Happy planning!

RISK MANAGEMENT IN CONTRACTING WORK

"Risk comes from not knowing what you're doing." - Warren Buffett

Identifying Potential Pitfalls

When you're diving into the world of contracting, especially in something as pivotal as electrical work, the terrain can be as tricky as rewiring a vintage chandelier. Getting it right isn't just about choosing the brightest bulb in the box; it's about sidestepping potential pitfalls that could zap your project's budget and timeline, leaving you in the dark. Let's illuminate some of the common risks associated with electrical contracting, discuss strategies to mitigate unexpected issues, and outline the legal concerns you should be aware of.

Common Electrical Contracting Risks

First off, the backbone of any savvy homeowner or business owner's strategy is recognising the risks at play. Electrical contracting carries its specific set of challenges. One major risk is the quality of workmanship. Substandard work can not only lead to immediate failures but also pose serious safety hazards, such as electrical fires or shocks. It's essential to ensure that the contractor you choose has a stellar track record and credible references.

Another frequent hiccup is project delays. These can be caused by a myriad of factors: unexpected structural issues in a building, delays in obtaining necessary materials, or even the sudden unavailability of key contractor team members due to illness or other commitments. Each day your project lags can mean loss of use and, in a business scenario, a potential loss of income.

Lastly, cost overruns can send shivers down anyone's spine. They often occur due to initially underestimated project scopes or unforeseen complications that require additional work and materials. This is where getting a detailed quote and a clear understanding of the project scope becomes vital.

Mitigating Unexpected Issues

Now, let's talk about dodging these curveballs. Mitigation begins with choosing the right contractor. This choice should never be purely budget-driven. Look for licensed and insured professionals with a robust portfolio of completed projects similar to yours. Don't shy away from conducting interviews and asking pointed questions about their approach to handling unexpected issues.

Once you've selected your contractor, clear and continuous communication is your best defence against project derailments. Establish regular check-ins and insist on a communication protocol should any aspects of the project change. This keeps you in the loop and in control, allowing you to make informed decisions quickly.

Another effective strategy is to have a well-outlined contract in place. This should include detailed project specifications, timelines, payment schedules, and clauses that address potential changes or additional charges. Also, consider including penalty clauses for delays and incentives for early completion to keep the project on track.

Legal Concerns

Navigating the legal landscape is as crucial as the electrical work itself. The first step is understanding the regulations and codes applicable in your area. Electrical work is heavily regulated due to its inherent risks, and compliance is non-negotiable. Ensure your contractor can pull all the necessary permits and handle inspections required to sign off on the work completed.

Another legal pitfall is the liability in the event of faults or accidents linked to the electrical work. This is where your contractor's insurance—more on that later—plays a crucial role. It's advisable to verify that your contractor has sufficient liability insurance that protects you from claims arising from injuries or damages.

Lastly, be aware of the warranty provisions that cover the work done. These legal guarantees ensure that any defects or issues within a set period post-completion are rectified without additional costs. Make sure these terms are spelled out in the contract, clear and fair.

By understanding these potential pitfalls and preparing for them, you place yourself in a position of strength, ready to guide your project to a successful, stress-free completion. Remember, the goal here isn't just to get the job done; it's to get it done right, with peace of mind intact. So, take these insights, strap on your project management helmet, and turn the power on your next electrical contracting venture.

Insurance and Assurance

Importance of Contractor Insurance

Let's dive straight into the deep end. When you're hiring a contractor, whether to fix a leaky tap or completely remodel your kitchen, you're not just buying a service, you're also buying peace of mind. And how do you secure that peace of mind? By ensuring that your contractor is well-covered by insurance.

Now, you might wonder, why is it so critical that your contractor has insurance? Imagine this: the contractor accidentally hits a main water pipe, causing extensive water damage to your property. Without the right insurance, the financial burden of repairing this damage could fall squarely on your shoulders. Not the scenario you want after a simple renovation, right?

Contractor insurance acts as a safety net not just for the contractor but for you as the homeowner or business owner. It's designed to cover liability in case of accidents, damages, or injuries that occur on your property during the execution of the work. This includes public liability insurance, which covers injury or damage claims made by third parties (like your nosy neighbour who might trip over a tool and sprain an ankle).

Make sure your contractor has comprehensive coverage that extends beyond the basic requirements. This might include cover for accidental damage to the property, and even potentially covering the cost of redoing the work if it's not up to scratch due to contractor errors. The last thing you want is to be left high and dry because someone else didn't take the proper precautions.

What Your Contractor's Policy Should Cover

So, we've established that insurance is a must. But what exactly should that insurance cover? Not all policies are created equal, and it's crucial that the insurance your contractor holds is robust enough to protect against all potential risks.

First off, you'll want to ensure that their policy includes public liability insurance, as mentioned. This is pretty much non-negotiable. It protects you from being liable for any injuries or damages that occur as a result of the contractor's work.

Next up, check for product liability insurance. This covers you against damages caused by faulty materials or equipment used by the contractor. Say, for instance, a newly installed ceiling fan plummets to your living room floor a week after installation due to faulty fixtures. Product liability insurance should have you covered.

Another key aspect is professional indemnity insurance. This comes into play if the work done is subpar or if the contractor provides erroneous advice leading to a financial loss. For example, if a contractor incorrectly installs solar panels leading to inefficiency and increased costs, you'd definitely want recourse.

Don't shy away from asking your contractor for a copy of their insurance certificates, and feel free to verify that with the insurance provider. It's perfectly reasonable—and responsible—to ensure that the coverage is active and adequate.

Your Own Home Insurance Considerations

While it's crucial for your contractor to have their insurance in check, don't overlook your own role in this two-player game. Your own home insurance needs a check-up to ensure you're adequately covered during and after the contracting work.

Before any work commences, get in touch with your home insurance provider. You need to inform them of the upcoming work and check if any aspects of the renovations could affect your current policy. Sometimes, major structural changes can potentially void existing policies if the insurer is not informed beforehand.

Moreover, some home insurance policies include a clause that covers any accidental damage during renovations. However, this can vary significantly between policies and providers. Clarifying this beforehand can save you a world of hassle in case something goes awry.

If the contracting work increases the value of your property, you might also need to consider adjusting your home insurance cover to reflect the increased value of your home. It's a good idea to reassess your policy once the work is complete to ensure that your coverage is adequate and reflects any new risks or values.

Additionally, if you're vacating your home during renovation, confirm that your home insurance covers the property while it's unoccupied. Some policies have specific conditions or reduced cover for unoccupied properties.

By ensuring both you and your contractor have the right insurance in place, you're not just protecting your property; you're also safeguarding your financial stability. Remember, contracting work involves certain risks, and while you can't eliminate these risks entirely, you can certainly manage them effectively through the right insurance strategies. This approach not only mitigates potential financial disasters but also ensures that the renovation process is smooth and stress-free. So, take the time to get this right – your peace of mind is worth it.

Safety First

When it comes to managing risk in contracting work, prioritising safety isn't just a good idea—it's essential. As you navigate through the complexities of hiring and working with contractors, understanding and implementing safety standards, establishing effective emergency protocols, and ensuring regular maintenance and checks are not just precautionary measures; they are your safeguards against potential disasters. Let's delve deeper into each aspect to ensure you're equipped to promote a safe working environment on your property.

Compliance with Safety Standards

First things first, ensuring that any contractor you hire complies with the relevant safety standards is a fundamental step. Depending on where you live, there are likely to be stringent regulations in place that govern all manner of construction and maintenance activities. These rules are not just bureaucratic red tape; they are crafted to protect both you and the workers from avoidable accidents and injuries.

For electrical work, for example, there are specific codes that must be followed to ensure everything is up to scratch. From the installation of new electrical systems to the maintenance of existing ones, these codes provide a guideline that, when followed, significantly reduces the risk of electrical fires or shocks. It's crucial that you ask your contractor about their adherence to such standards right from the outset. Don't just take their word for it either; ask for proof. This could be in the form of certifications or accreditations from recognised industry bodies.

Moreover, if the contracting work involves areas like asbestos removal or working at heights, the stakes are even higher. These activities require additional certifications and training. Ensuring your contractor's team is properly trained and equipped not only keeps them safe, it also minimises your liability as the property owner in case something goes wrong.

Emergency Protocols

No matter how well you plan and how many precautions you take, emergencies can still happen. That's why having robust emergency protocols in place is crucial. Your contractor should be able to provide you with a clear, detailed plan outlining what steps to take in various emergency scenarios. This includes accidents, sudden equipment failures, or unexpected discoveries like finding hazardous materials during renovations.

Ask your contractor about their emergency response plan before work begins. This plan should include contact information for all relevant parties, including the local emergency services, a list of all team members on site with their roles clearly defined, and a communication plan to inform you of any incidents.

You should also discuss and agree upon a clear evacuation route for all types of emergencies, which should be marked clearly and known to all workers and occupants of the building. Regular drills, although often overlooked, can make a big difference in emergency situations. They ensure everyone knows exactly what to do and where to go, which can significantly reduce panic and confusion, thereby preventing further injuries.

Regular Maintenance and Checks

Last but certainly not least, regular maintenance and periodic checks are vital. This is particularly relevant for long-term projects but is equally important for any size of job. Regular checks help in identifying potential problems before they turn into serious issues. For instance, ensuring that all equipment is in good working order can prevent malfunctions that might cause delays or accidents.

Moreover, regular site audits can help ensure ongoing compliance with both safety standards and your initial project specifications. These audits can be conducted by independent safety consultants or qualified members of the contractor's team, depending on the project's complexity and the risks involved. The key here is consistency; these checks should be scheduled at regular intervals and not just at the project's commencement and conclusion.

Maintenance extends beyond the machinery and equipment. It also involves keeping the site clean and organised. A cluttered workspace can increase the risk of accidents, such as trips and falls, and can complicate evacuation efforts in an emergency. Ensure your contractor has a system in place to manage waste and to keep the work area tidy.

In conclusion, managing safety in contracting work requires a proactive approach. By ensuring compliance with safety standards, establishing effective emergency protocols, and insisting on regular maintenance and checks, you not only safeguard the workers and your property but also contribute to the overall success of your project. Remember, cutting corners on safety can have far-reaching consequences, so it's always better to be safe than sorry.

RECAP AND ACTION ITEMS

Wrapping up our deep dive into the world of risk management in contracting work, you now have the toolkit to navigate the potential minefields of your next project. From identifying the usual suspects of pitfalls in electrical contracting to understanding the nitty-gritty of insurance and ensuring compliance with safety standards, you're much better equipped.

So, what's next? It's all about putting this knowledge into action to protect your interests and ensure a smooth project execution.

1. **Review and Verify Contractor Credentials**: Before signing on the dotted line, make sure your contractor is not only reputable but also has the necessary qualifications and insurance. Check their references and past work. This isn't about doubting their capabilities, but ensuring they meet the high standards your project deserves.

2. **Insurance Checklist**: Create a checklist of the insurance coverage your contractor should have. This includes general liability, workers' compensation, and any other relevant policies. Ask to see proof of insurance and consider getting additional

advice from an insurance advisor to review the policies if you're unsure.

3. **Document Everything:** From the initial agreement to every change and discussion about the project, keep a written record. This will not only help in managing the project more effectively but will also serve as vital documentation if any legal issue arises.

4. **Safety Audit:** Before work begins, conduct a safety audit of the site with your contractor. Ensure that all compliance measures are in place and discuss the emergency protocols. Regularly schedule these checks throughout the project duration to maintain a safe working environment.

5. **Regular Maintenance:** Post-project, don't just breathe a sigh of relief. Set up a schedule for regular maintenance checks, especially for critical areas like electrical systems. This proactive step can save you from future hassles and unexpected repair costs.

By taking these steps, you can minimise risk and position your project on a trajectory towards success. Remember, effective risk management in contracting isn't just about avoiding problems; it's about creating a framework that allows for peace of mind and ensures that the project runs smoothly from start to finish.

THE ART OF NEGOTIATION WITH A SINGLE CONTRACTOR

"The most important thing in communication is hearing what isn't said." - Peter Drucker

Preparing to Negotiate

Negotiation can sometimes feel like you're trying to defuse a bomb under pressure, but it doesn't have to be this way. With the right preparation, you can approach negotiations with confidence, ensuring you get the best value and service. Let's dive into how you can prepare effectively.

Understanding Market Rates

Before you even make the initial phone call or send that probing email, you need to understand what the going rate is for the service or product you're seeking. Imagine walking into a negotiation without this knowledge—it's like stepping into a game of darts blindfolded.

Start with a bit of detective work. The internet is your best friend here. Look for pricing information on websites, forums, and even social media groups related to your project. Don't shy away from calling up service providers—posing as a prospective client—to get a quote directly. This isn't just about getting the lowest price; it's about understanding the full landscape of pricing so that you can recognise a fair offer when you see one.

In addition to digital sleuthing, tap into your network. Speak with friends, family, or colleagues who have recently undertaken similar projects. They can provide insights not just on what they paid, but also on any hidden costs they encountered. This real-world data is invaluable.

Once you've gathered this information, create a range. Have a clear idea of the highest and lowest market rates. This range will serve as your benchmark for what is reasonable and will empower you to negotiate from a position of strength.

Clarity on Your Project Needs

Knowing exactly what you want is half the battle in any negotiation. Begin by outlining the scope of your project in detail. What are the must-haves and what are the nice-to-haves? By defining the scope, you can avoid the common pitfall of scope creep, which can lead to increased costs and extended timelines.

Write down your requirements and if possible, break them down into phases. This not only makes your project more manageable but also makes it easier for the contractor to provide an accurate quote. Be as specific as possible about materials, finishes, and the expected timeline. Remember, ambiguity breeds confusion and can dilute your negotiating position.

This clarity also helps in communicating your vision to the contractor. When both parties understand what is expected, there's less room for misunderstanding, which can often lead to disputes.

Setting Your Negotiation Boundaries

Before you enter into negotiations, it's crucial to set your boundaries. Decide beforehand what your deal breakers are. These are the conditions under which you would walk away from a deal. It might be a certain price point, timeline, or a specific aspect of service delivery. Knowing your limits is empowering and keeps you from making decisions that you might regret later.

Equally important is knowing your flexibility points. These are areas where you can afford to give a little to get a little. Perhaps there's a non-essential feature of the project you can do without, or maybe you can extend the timeline if it means a decrease in cost.

Set these boundaries with a clear mind and a focus on your ultimate goal. Remember, the aim of negotiation is not to defeat the other party, but to reach an agreement that benefits both sides. This preparation ensures that you enter negotiations with a firm understanding of your needs and limits, which is essential for effective bargaining.

By the end of this preparatory phase, you should feel equipped with the knowledge of what's reasonable to ask for and what's not. You'll know the market rates, have a clear project plan, and understand your boundaries. This isn't just preparation; it's arming yourself with the tools needed for successful negotiation. So take these steps seriously, as they set the stage for the negotiation tactics you will employ in your discussions with the contractor.

Effective Communication Techniques

Mastering communication is like learning to dance gracefully with words. When you're knee-deep in negotiations with a contractor, the difference between a stumble and a pirouette can come down to how well you convey your thoughts and how attentively you listen. Let's break down the essentials to turn you into a communication virtuoso.

Building a Rapport

Imagine walking into a negotiation with someone you like and trust. Feels less like a battlefield, right? Building rapport isn't about manipulating emotions; it's about fostering a genuine connection that can lead to better understanding and cooperation.

Start by finding common ground. Maybe you and the contractor both love dogs, or perhaps you've discovered that you both started your businesses around the same time. Whatever it is, use it as a stepping stone to create a friendly atmosphere. Remember, people are more willing to negotiate and compromise with someone they find agreeable and respectful.

Next, appreciate their expertise. Contractors take pride in their skills and knowledge. Recognise their professionalism by asking thoughtful questions about their work and listening intently to their answers. This not only shows that you value their opinion but also helps you understand their perspective, making it easier to align your expectations.

Lastly, keep your interactions positive. Even if the negotiation becomes challenging, maintaining a polite and optimistic tone can prevent the conversation from turning sour. A smile, a bit of humour, and a positive attitude can go a long way in keeping the dialogue productive.

Clear and Concise Requests

When it comes to discussing what you need, clarity is king. You want to avoid misunderstandings that can lead to frustration and added costs. Begin by being specific about your project requirements. Instead of saying, "I want a modern kitchen," provide details like, "I'm looking for a kitchen with quartz countertops, under-cabinet lighting, and a central island."

Use simple language. While it's tempting to use technical terms or jargon to appear well-informed, it's crucial that your contractor clearly understands your requests. If there's any ambiguity, it can lead to incorrect assumptions and results that don't meet your expectations.

Be concise but thorough. Don't overwhelm your contractor with unnecessary information, but make sure you've covered all the essentials. It's like packing for a holiday – bring everything you need without overloading your suitcase.

Always summarise your key points at the end of your discussion to ensure both you and the contractor are on the same page. This recap can help reinforce understanding and show the contractor that you are organised and serious about your project.

Listening Skills

Negotiation is a two-way street. While expressing your own needs is vital, actively listening to your contractor is equally important. It shows respect and allows you to grasp fully their concerns, limitations, and suggestions.

Practice active listening by focusing entirely on the speaker. Avoid the temptation to think about your next point while the contractor is talking. Instead, listen to understand, not just to reply. Nodding occasionally, maintaining eye contact, and repeating back what you've heard are all techniques that demonstrate you are engaged and value what they have to say.

Be open to their expertise. Contractors might suggest alternatives that could save you money or enhance the quality of the project. By being receptive to their suggestions, you could discover options you hadn't considered.

Finally, ask open-ended questions. These require more than a yes or no answer and encourage the contractor to share comprehensive information. Questions like "What do you think would be the best approach for this project?" or "Can you explain more about that technique?" can provide insights into their thought process and help clarify details.

By mastering these communication techniques, you ensure that your negotiation is not just an exchange of demands but a collaborative effort to achieve a common goal. Remember, successful negotiation is not about winning a battle; it's about finding a solution that satisfies both parties, creating a win-win scenario. So put these strategies into practice, and watch how they transform your interactions with your contractor into opportunities for success.

Sealing the Deal

Agreeing on terms can often feel like the most challenging part of the negotiation process, but it's where the magic happens. It's the culmination of all your preparation and effective communication. Now, you're so close to transforming your project vision into a tangible agreement. Here's how you can navigate through this crucial phase.

Agreeing on Terms

Firstly, it's imperative to ensure that both you and your contractor are entirely clear on what has been discussed so far. It's not just about being on the same page; it's about understanding each other's expectations down to the smallest detail. Begin by summarising what you've understood from your interactions. This recap isn't just for you—it helps the contractor see that you've been attentive and value their input.

Once both parties agree on the summary, you can move to lay down the final terms. This is where your earlier preparation on market rates and project needs pays off. You'll be able to justify your stance with data and clear reasoning, which makes it easier for the contractor to understand your perspective rather than seeing it as a hardball tactic.

Negotiation is often seen as a battle, but try viewing it as a process of aligning interests. Your contractor wants the job, and you want your project done to a specific standard and within a budget. There's common ground there – find it. If there are sticking points, don't hesitate to explore creative solutions like phased payments, performance bonuses, or adjusted timelines which can help both parties feel they are getting a fair deal.

Remember, clarity is key. Every aspect of the agreement should be transparent and agreed upon by both parties. This prevents potential misunderstandings or resentments that could surface later.

Contract Essentials

The importance of a well-drafted contract cannot be overstated. It's your safeguard, your point of reference, and essentially the rulebook by which your project will be executed. The contract should clearly state everything from the scope of work and materials to be used, to timelines and payment schedules. It should also clearly outline the responsibilities of each party.

Make sure that the contract includes clauses on how to handle any unforeseen circumstances. What happens if there is a delay due to weather, or if there is a sudden unavailability of specified materials? Planning for such scenarios in your contract will save you a lot of potential stress and disagreement down the line.

Also, consider including a clause that outlines the process for changes to the work agreed upon. It's not uncommon for projects to evolve, and you'll want a predefined way of dealing with changes without causing disputes or confusion.

Engaging a legal professional to either draft or review your contract can be a wise investment. Yes, it is an added cost, but think of it as buying peace of mind. You'll know that your interests are protected and that you're not inadvertently agreeing to terms that could cause problems later.

Handling Disagreements Professionally

Even with the best-laid plans, disagreements can occur. It's how you handle these disagreements that can make the difference between a project that is temporarily off track and one that derails completely.

First, always approach disagreements with a mindset to resolve rather than to win. Keep your communication lines open and try to understand the contractor's perspective. Often, disagreements arise from miscommunications or different interpretations of the same facts. A calm, clear conversation can usually clear up such misunderstandings.

If the disagreement escalates, refer back to your contract. It should be your primary guide in resolving disputes. Look at the terms agreed upon about handling conflicts and follow them. If it involves mediation or arbitration, be prepared to follow through with these steps.

Sometimes, bringing in a third party like a mediator can help offer a neutral perspective and facilitate a resolution. Remember, the goal is to complete your project successfully, not to stretch out conflicts or create animosity.

In all of this, maintain professionalism. Keep your interactions respectful and focused on solutions. This maintains a positive working relationship and helps ensure that the project gets back on track.

By carefully navigating the agreement process, ensuring all

contract details are ironed out, and handling any disagreements professionally, you're setting up your project for success. It's not just about getting the work done; it's about achieving your vision in a way that respects both your interests and those of your contractor. This approach not only leads to better project outcomes but builds relationships that can prove valuable for future projects.

RECAP AND ACTION ITEMS

Congratulations! You've just taken a deep dive into the art of negotiating with a single contractor. By now, you should feel equipped with the knowledge to confidently prepare for your negotiations, communicate effectively, and seal the deal smoothly.

Let's quickly recap the essential points. First, you've understood the importance of being prepared. Knowing the market rates and having a clear vision of your project, along with well-defined boundaries, sets the stage for a successful negotiation. Next, your ability to build rapport, make clear and concise requests, and listen actively have undoubtedly enhanced your communication skills, making it easier to connect and negotiate with contractors. Finally, agreeing on terms, understanding the essentials of a good contract, and handling disagreements professionally are crucial to finalising any agreement confidently and ensuring both parties are satisfied.

Now, it's time to put this knowledge into action. Here are some practical steps to take as you move forward with your project:

1. **Research Market Rates**: Before your next meeting, spend some time online or talk to industry experts to get an idea of the current market rates for your project. This will give you a benchmark for negotiations.

2. **Document Your Project Needs**: Write a clear, detailed description of your project, including budgets, timelines, and expected outcomes. This will serve as your guideline during discussions and ensure you don't stray from your primary objectives.

3. **Practice Your Communication Skills**: Try role-playing a negotiation with a friend or colleague. This practice can help you refine how you express your needs and respond to counteroffers.

4. **Prepare a Contract Template**: Have a basic contract template ready that outlines general terms and conditions. This can be customised according to your specific agreements, saving you time and providing a legal safeguard.

5. **Develop a Disagreement Management Plan**: Think about potential disagreements that could arise and how you would handle them. Having a plan will keep you calm and professional if things don't go as expected.

Remember, negotiation is not just about getting the best price; it's about creating value for both parties. It's a partnership that, when done well, can lead to more successful and fulfilling outcomes. Good luck, and may your negotiations be smooth and fruitful!

LEVERAGING TECHNOLOGY IN MODERN CONTRACTING

"The best way to predict the future is to invent it." – *Alan Kay*

Technological Advancements in Electrical Contracting

In the realm of electrical contracting, the pace of technological evolution is not just rapid; it's revolutionary. The industry today bears little resemblance to its former self, largely due to advancements in tools, software, and energy-efficient technologies. Embracing these innovations can streamline your projects, reduce costs, and enhance efficiency. Here's how you can leverage the latest breakthroughs to ensure your electrical needs are not just met but exceeded.

Latest Tools and Equipment

The toolbox of today's electrical contractor looks vastly different from that of a decade ago. Modern tools are designed to improve accuracy, safety, and speed. For instance, laser and GPS technologies are now commonplace in measuring and layout tools, allowing for precision that was previously unattainable. Imagine a scenario where you need to install an intricate lighting system across your new office complex; laser-guided tools can ensure every light is perfectly aligned, without the usual trial and error.

Another significant advancement is the use of thermal imaging cameras. These devices allow electricians to see beyond the limitations of the human eye, identifying potential electrical faults before they become major issues. This means that you can prevent downtime or dangerous situations, such as electrical fires, well before they pose a real threat.

Robotic tools, though more of an investment, are making their way into larger scale operations. These robots can pull cables through conduits, significantly reducing the manpower needed and protecting workers from potential injuries associated with manual pulling. While the upfront cost might be higher, the long-term savings in labour and enhanced safety can be well worth it.

Software for Project Management

Gone are the days of managing electrical projects with pen and paper. Today, a variety of software solutions exist that can help you handle everything from scheduling to invoicing with unprecedented ease and accuracy. Project management software tailored for electrical contractors can integrate aspects such as design, cost estimation, and project timelines into one streamlined interface.

For instance, software now allows for real-time updates. If a project detail changes, it's immediately reflected across all aspects of the project plan. This means fewer mistakes, less miscommunication, and a much smoother operational flow. You and your team can access project details from anywhere, be it on a laptop at the office or a mobile device onsite.

Additionally, such software often includes features for customer relationship management (CRM). This can be a game changer for maintaining and analysing customer interactions, helping you to build stronger relationships and, ultimately, a more robust business reputation.

Energy-efficient Technologies

In today's world, energy efficiency is not just a buzzword but a business strategy. Advances in energy-efficient technologies not only help save on costs but also appeal to the growing market of environmentally conscious consumers.

One of the standout innovations in this area is LED lighting technology. LEDs are vastly more efficient than traditional incandescent bulbs and have a longer lifespan. They reduce the amount of energy used for lighting, which can significantly decrease electricity bills. Moreover, they are less prone to malfunctions, thereby reducing maintenance costs.

Another area where technology is making big strides is in

the integration of renewable energy sources like solar panels. Modern electrical contracting increasingly involves setting up these systems, which can be connected to the grid to supply excess power and possibly even generate revenue.

Furthermore, smart systems are now capable of more efficiently managing the energy consumption of an entire building or set of buildings. These systems use sensors and IoT (Internet of Things) technology to automatically adjust lighting, heating, and cooling based on real-time occupancy and weather conditions. This not only ensures optimal comfort but also maximises energy efficiency without requiring manual intervention.

Incorporating these technologies into your projects not only makes them cutting-edge but also ensures they are sustainable and cost-effective in the long run. The initial investment in energy-efficient technologies is quickly offset by the savings in energy costs and the potential for government rebates and incentives.

As you step into your next electrical project, consider how these technological advancements can be integrated. Whether it's the precision of modern tools, the organisational prowess of project management software, or the sustainability of energy-efficient technologies, each plays a pivotal role in modernising and enhancing electrical contracting services.

Online Tools for Contractor Verification

In the maze of modern contracting, where the stakes are both high and hidden beneath layers of complexity, you've got to be a step ahead when verifying the credibility of your potential contractors. The digital age, thankfully, serves up some nifty tools designed to streamline this process. From plumbing the depths of online databases to tapping into the wellspring of trade association resources, the ways to ensure you're hiring the right person for the job are at your fingertips.

Using Online Databases

Imagine having a digital detective at your disposal, one that can sift through the clutter and zero in on the information that matters most. That's what online databases can do for you when you're on the hunt for a reliable contractor. These platforms are vast repositories of data, offering insights into the professional lives of contractors across the country.

For starters, there's the simplicity of access. With a few clicks, you can enter a contractor's name or company into a search field and pull up a detailed history of their professional undertakings. These databases often include past project portfolios, customer reviews, and sometimes even details of legal disputes or complaints lodged against them.

But it's not just about digging up the dirt. These resources can also highlight a contractor's strengths, showcasing areas where they excel. Look for platforms that provide a balanced view to get a full spectrum understanding of who you're dealing with.

Remember, though, while these tools are powerful, they're not infallible. Cross-referencing information from multiple sources can help you build a more accurate picture. Use them as a starting point to guide your deeper investigations.

Assessing Reviews

Now, let's delve into public opinion: reviews. Online reviews are a crucial tool for gaining insights into a contractor's reliability, punctuality, work ethic, and how they interact with clients. These firsthand accounts can paint a realistic picture of what it's like to work with a particular contractor.

Exercise discernment when reviewing feedback. Understand that not all reviews may be unbiased or entirely accurate. Look for recurring themes and patterns across multiple reviews, which can provide a more reliable indication of the contractor's performance and professionalism.

In addition to reviews, consider exploring other sources of information, such as testimonials from acquaintances or industry peers, to gather a well-rounded perspective. Combining these insights will help you make a more informed decision when selecting a contractor for your project.

Utilising Trade Association Resources

Trade associations are often overlooked treasure troves of information and validation for contractors. Membership in a reputable trade association can be a sign of a contractor's commitment to their craft and adherence to industry standards.

These associations typically have strict criteria for membership, including certain levels of professionalism, adherence to ethical codes, and ongoing education. By consulting a trade association's website, you can confirm whether a contractor is a member in good standing, which adds an extra layer of credibility to their profile.

Moreover, these associations often provide mediation and arbitration services in case of disputes, which offers you an additional safety net. They can also be a source of up-to-date industry news and developments, helping you understand innovations and standards that your contractor should be aware of.

When you're navigating the labyrinth of contractor verification, think of these online tools as your digital compasses. Online databases, licensing checks, reviews, and trade association resources—they collectively form a robust arsenal in your quest to secure a trustworthy contractor. By methodically using these tools, you empower yourself with knowledge, and in the realm of contracting, knowledge not only equates to power but also peace of mind.

Smart Homes and Electrical Needs

Up-to-Date with Modern Needs

In the realm of modern living, keeping your home's electrical systems synchronised with the latest technology isn't just a luxury—it's an essential step towards efficient and comfortable living. As you navigate the evolving landscape of home automation, understanding the role of advanced electrical frameworks becomes crucial.

Imagine controlling your lighting, heating, and security systems all from a swipe on your smartphone. It's not the stuff of sci-fi anymore; it's what modern homes are made of. But to harness this convenience, your home's electrical infrastructure must be robust and adaptable. Upgrading to smart-ready electrical panels, incorporating IoT (Internet of Things) compatible outlets, and ensuring your wiring can handle increased loads is just the start.

The importance here is not just in adding value to your property—it's about crafting a living space that responds to your needs and lifestyle effortlessly. Integrating smart technologies means installing energy-efficient appliances that can communicate with one another, optimising usage and reducing unnecessary waste. For instance, smart thermostats adjust the heating based on your daily schedule and weather predictions, offering both comfort and cost savings.

Special Considerations for Smart Homes

Transitioning to a smart home isn't merely about purchasing new gadgets; it requires a deep understanding of the compatibility between new technologies and existing electrical systems. One major consideration is the surge in power usage. Smart devices, while individually not power-hungry, cumulatively increase the demand on your electrical system. This is where updated wiring and possibly even a new circuit panel come into play to handle this load without tripping breakers.

Another key aspect is the integration complexity. Unlike traditional setups, smart home devices often need to be interconnected, requiring a central hub or controller that can communicate across different platforms. This is where professional expertise shines. Electing contractors who are well-versed in smart technology installations becomes indispensable. They can ensure that all components function seamlessly together, avoiding the common pitfalls of DIY installations such as incompatible device communication or incorrect wiring that could lead to system failures.

Moreover, security takes on a new dimension in smart homes. With most devices connected to the internet, your home becomes potentially vulnerable to cyber threats. Ensuring robust security protocols, like advanced encryption for data transfers between your devices and continuous software updates, is fundamental. Here, again, the expertise of knowledgeable contractors can help you navigate the complexities of secure smart home setups, ensuring that convenience does not compromise safety.

Long-Term Benefits of Advanced Setups

Investing in advanced electrical setups for your smart home goes beyond immediate comfort and enters the realm of long-term benefits. Firstly, the energy efficiency aspect is transformative. Smart homes are adept at using energy only when it's needed, significantly reducing your utility bills. Automated lights, climate control systems that adjust according to occupancy and time of day, and intelligently managed power systems contribute to a smaller carbon footprint.

Future-proofing your property is another significant advantage. As technology evolves, having an adaptable system means you can integrate newer innovations without major overhauls. This adaptability not only enhances your home's functionality but also increases its market value, making it a compelling feature if you decide to sell.

Finally, the quality of life improvements cannot be overstated. Imagine waking up to a gradually brightening light that simulates sunrise, or returning home to a pre-warmed living room in the winter—all automated to your preferences. These convenances become everyday realities with a well-designed smart electrical system.

In conclusion, as you consider upgrading your home to smart standards, think of it not just in terms of adding gadgets but as an overall enhancement of your living environment. The electrical needs of modern smart homes are complex, but with the right setup, the benefits—ranging from increased convenience and security to energy efficiency and improved property value—are immense. Choosing the right contractor to guide you through this process is critical; their expertise will ensure that your home is not only equipped to handle today's technology but is also prepared for tomorrow's innovations.

RECAP AND ACTION ITEMS

As you've explored the realm of modern contracting, harnessing technology is not just an option; it's essential for efficiency, reliability, and ensuring the most up-to-date solutions for your electrical needs. From the latest in tools and equipment that streamline operations to sophisticated software managing projects from start to finish, technology empowers you to make informed decisions. Additionally, transitioning towards energy-efficient technologies not only optimises your electrical usage but significantly cuts down on costs, contributing to a healthier planet.

Navigating the maze of finding reliable contractors can be daunting. However, with the advent of online resources, the verification process has been simplified. Databases provide a treasure trove of information on contractors, allowing you to sift through qualifications, license statuses, and real customer reviews. Moreover, tapping into trade associations can offer added reassurance and resources tailored to your specific requirements.

The push towards smart homes has introduced a plethora of new electrical demands. Staying abreast of these advancements ensures that your home or business is equipped for the future, enhancing functionality while maximising security and convenience. The investment in smart technology today spells substantial savings and peace of mind tomorrow.

Here are some actionable steps to take your understanding into practical application:

1. **Assess your current systems**: Assess your existing electrical systems and identify areas where upgrades could increase efficiency and safety.

2. **Research and Reach Out**: Utilise online databases and resources to find qualified, reputable contractors. Don't hesitate to contact trade associations for further insights and recommendations.

3. **Embrace Smart Solutions**: If upgrading, consider integrating smart home technologies. Consult with experts to tailor these systems to your specific needs, ensuring compatibility and scalability.

4. **Plan for the Future**: As you upgrade, think long-term. Opt for solutions that offer flexibility and adaptability as technology evolves.

5. **Stay Informed**: Keep abreast of new developments in technology that could impact your electrical setups. Regular updates could mean timely enhancements to your systems.

By integrating these technologies and strategies, you ensure that your property remains at the cutting edge, not only increasing its value but also enhancing your quality of life and work. Dive into these advancements with confidence and watch as they pay off in efficiency, safety, and satisfaction.

SUSTAINABLE PRACTICES AND YOUR ELECTRICAL NEEDS

"The greatest threat to our planet is the belief that someone else will save it." - Robert Swan

Eco-Friendly Electrical Solutions

In an era where sustainability isn't just a buzzword but a necessity, shifting your focus to eco-friendly electrical solutions could be one of the most impactful decisions you make—not just for the environment, but for your peace of mind and your pocket. Let's delve into the myriad benefits these green choices offer, from the tangible gains of employing sustainable materials to the broader implications of reducing your carbon footprint.

Benefits of Green Energy Solutions

You've probably heard a lot about green energy solutions. Solar panels gleaming on rooftops and wind turbines spinning in the distance are becoming part of our landscape. But what do these technologies mean for you personally?

First and foremost, integrating renewable energy sources like solar, wind, or even geothermal systems into your home or business isn't just good for the planet—it's good for your energy bills. By harnessing the power of nature, you can significantly reduce dependence on non-renewable energy sources, which are subject to market fluctuations and, frankly, are dwindling.

Moreover, the use of these technologies can often qualify you for governmental incentives. Tax credits, rebates, and grants are available in many regions to offset initial installation costs. This not only accelerates the return on your investment but also underscores the communal push towards sustainable living.

Renewable energy sources also come with the added benefit of predictability. While traditional energy prices can spike due to various factors, the 'fuel' for your solar panels or wind turbines is always free and abundantly available. This stability can be particularly comforting in today's volatile market environment.

Sustainable Materials in Electrical Work

When it comes to eco-friendly electrical solutions, it's not just the source of energy that matters but also the materials used in your systems. Sustainable materials in electrical work are those that are sourced, processed, and applied in a manner that reduces their environmental impact.

Copper, often used in wiring, is a good example. It's not

only highly efficient in conducting electricity but also 100% recyclable without any loss of quality. This means that the copper used in your electrical installations could potentially have had past lives in other applications and can continue to be used in the future without harming the environment.

Another aspect to consider is the insulation of electrical cables. Materials such as thermoplastic elastomer (TPE) are becoming popular as sustainable alternatives to PVC. TPEs are not only recyclable but also require less energy to produce and process, and they emit fewer toxic materials during production and disposal.

By choosing materials that are durable and recyclable, you contribute to a reduction in waste and resource consumption. This not only helps in conserving the environment but also aligns with global efforts to transition to a circular economy.

Reducing Carbon Footprint

Your carbon footprint is essentially a measure of the impact your activities have on the environment, particularly in terms of the amount of greenhouse gases produced, measured in units of carbon dioxide. By opting for eco-friendly electrical solutions, you're taking a significant step towards reducing this footprint.

The implementation of energy-efficient appliances is a straight-forward start. These devices consume less power for the same level of performance as their less efficient counterparts, meaning they reduce the amount of energy you need to draw from the grid, which in turn reduces your carbon emissions.

Another effective strategy is to improve home insulation. Better insulation means less energy is needed for heating and cooling, which not only lowers energy consumption but also enhances the overall efficiency of your renewable energy systems, should you have them installed.

Lastly, consider the impact of LED lighting. LEDs use at least 75% less energy than incandescent lighting and last 25 times longer. By switching to LED, you're not only cutting down on your energy use and costs but also on waste and replacement frequency.

Each of these choices contributes to a smaller carbon footprint. When combined, they represent a comprehensive approach to reducing your personal and business impact on the environment. This not only helps in slowing down climate change but also promotes a healthier lifestyle and, potentially, a cleaner conscience.

By embracing these eco-friendly electrical solutions, you're not just setting up systems that save you money and increase your property's efficiency; you're participating in a larger, global movement towards sustainability. This shift can make a substantial difference in how you impact the world and how you perceive your role within it.

Long-Term Sustainability

When considering any form of investment in your property, the durability and longevity of the solutions you choose are paramount. In the realm of eco-friendly electrical systems, this takes on an added dimension. Not only do you want systems that last and function efficiently, but you also need them to be sustainable and gentle on the planet over the long haul.

Durability and Maintenance

Imagine installing a system that not only powers your home or business efficiently but also stands the test of time with minimal fuss. That's the dual promise of sustainable electrical solutions. Traditionally, electrical systems require ongoing maintenance to ensure efficiency and safety. However, eco-friendly systems are often designed with durability at their core.

Take, for example, solar panels. These are not just effective in harnessing natural energy but are also built to withstand harsh weather conditions, from scorching sun to battering rains. Most solar panels come with a warranty of 20 to 25 years, but they can last much longer if maintained properly. It's not just about the longevity of the panels themselves but also about the inverters and storage batteries, which are getting better and more durable by the day.

LED lighting is another brilliant example. Unlike traditional bulbs, LEDs can last up to 25 times longer and use at least 75%

less energy. When you switch to LED, you're not just cutting down on your energy usage; you're also reducing the frequency of replacements, thereby minimising waste and maintenance costs.

Maintaining these systems often requires less effort than traditional setups. Many modern sustainable technologies come equipped with monitoring systems that provide real-time data on performance and potential issues, allowing for preemptive maintenance. This can significantly reduce the downtime and the hit-and-miss nature of older systems where problems were often only discovered after a failure.

Cost-effectiveness of Sustainable Solutions

While the initial outlay for green energy solutions might feel steep, the long-term cost savings are substantial. The key here is to look beyond the upfront costs and focus on the lifecycle costs of these systems. Sustainable electrical solutions often pay for themselves over time through reduced energy bills and maintenance costs.

For instance, the upfront installation cost of solar panels can be offset by the savings on your electricity bills. In many regions, you can also benefit from government incentives and rebates designed to encourage the adoption of renewable energy. Additionally, as energy prices continue to rise, the relative savings over time can increase significantly.

Moreover, when you invest in high-quality, durable solutions, the need for replacements and extensive repairs diminishes. This aspect of sustainability not only saves money but also reduces the environmental impact associated with manufacturing, transporting, and disposing of electrical components.

Impact on Property Value

In today's eco-conscious market, greener homes and businesses are not just a luxury but a growing expectation. Properties equipped with sustainable electrical systems often attract a premium in the real estate market. Homebuyers and business investors are increasingly aware of the benefits of eco-friendly installations, both in terms of cost savings and environmental impact.

A study by the UK's Energy Saving Trust found that energy-efficient homes can fetch a higher price on the market. Features like double-glazing, energy-efficient heating systems, and solar panels are seen as valuable additions. For businesses, sustainable practices can boost your brand's image, attract eco-conscious customers, and provide a competitive edge in an increasingly green marketplace.

Furthermore, properties with sustainable solutions meet more stringent regulatory standards, which can be a significant advantage as governments tighten building regulations to meet climate targets. Compliance with these standards not only ensures you avoid potential fines but also positions your property as a future-proof investment.

Working with Contractors Who Value Sustainability

Identifying Eco-Conscious Contractors

When you're diving into the sea of potential contractors for your electrical needs, finding those who genuinely value sustainability can feel like hunting for a needle in a haystack. But fear not, it's not as daunting as it seems if you know what to look for.

First things first, certification and memberships can be a solid indicator of a contractor's commitment to sustainable practices. Look for those who boast credentials from recognized green organizations like the Green Building Council or similar local entities. These certifications aren't just fancy stickers on their profiles; they represent a contractor's dedication to upholding certain environmental standards in their projects.

Moreover, don't hesitate to dive deep during your initial discussions. Ask pointed questions about their past projects and specifically about the sustainable methods they employed. How do they manage waste? What materials do they recommend and why? Their answers will give you clear insights into how deeply ingrained sustainability is in their operational ethos.

Another pro tip is to check out their portfolio or case studies. Companies that prioritise eco-friendly methods will likely showcase these projects proudly. This not only gives you a peek into their capabilities but also illustrates their experience in integrating sustainable solutions in a practical, effective manner.

Collaborating on Green Initiatives

Once you've pinned down a contractor who ticks all the boxes for sustainability, the next step is to ensure that your project aligns with these green standards throughout its execution. Collaboration is key here. You need to be on the same page to make sure your sustainable vision translates seamlessly from paper to reality.

Start by setting clear, mutual goals at the very beginning. Whether it's achieving a specific energy efficiency rating or using a certain percentage of recycled materials, having these targets in place guides the project's trajectory right from the start. It's like setting the GPS before you start the drive – it makes the journey smoother and quicker.

Communication is your best friend in this phase. Regular meetings, whether face-to-face or virtual, help keep everything on track. Use these sessions not just for updates but also for brainstorming. Often, contractors who are passionate about sustainability are brimming with innovative ideas that could enhance your project's green quotient even further. Encourage this flow of creativity; it's a win-win.

And remember, collaboration goes beyond just talking. It involves actively listening and sometimes compromising. If your contractor suggests an alternative material or method that's more sustainable, consider it seriously—even if it wasn't part of your original plan. These adjustments can often lead to better outcomes, both for the environment and for the project's overall success.

Encouraging Sustainable Practices

Encouraging doesn't just mean giving a thumbs up from the sidelines; it means being actively involved in promoting sustainable practices throughout your project's lifecycle. How can you do this? By incentivising green choices.

Consider integrating a clause in your contract that rewards the contractor for achieving or exceeding sustainability targets. This could be in the form of a bonus or even public recognition of their efforts through your networks or social media platforms. Positive reinforcement goes a long way in not just meeting but surpassing goals.

Moreover, be open to learning and adopting new sustainability practices yourself. Sometimes, you might find that what you initially thought was the 'greenest' option available might have been superseded by newer, more effective solutions. Stay flexible and open to adopting these innovations, even if it means steering away slightly from your pre-planned path.

Lastly, spread the word. When you find a contractor who truly prioritises sustainability and delivers exceptional results, shout about it from the rooftops. Your endorsement not only helps them gain more like-minded clients but also sets a benchmark in the industry for others to follow. In doing so, you're not just completing your project; you're also contributing to a larger movement towards sustainability in the construction and electrical industries.

By carefully selecting your contractor, collaborating closely on green goals, and encouraging ongoing sustainable practices, you are ensuring that your electrical needs are met in a way that aligns with your environmental values. It's about creating a partnership that not only enlightens but also empowers the shift towards a more sustainable future.

RECAP AND ACTION ITEMS

As you've explored the facets of sustainable electrical practices, you now have a solid grounding in how green energy solutions can enhance your environment and contribute significantly towards a sustainable future. The journey from understanding the benefits of sustainable materials in electrical work to identifying and collaborating with eco-conscious contractors, positions you perfectly to make informed decisions that align with your values of sustainability and efficiency.

To move forward from here, begin by reviewing your current electrical setup and identifying areas where eco-friendly solutions can be introduced. Consider the following action steps:

1. **Audit Your Energy Use:** Start by having an energy audit conducted on your property. This will highlight the most energy-intensive areas and suggest the most immediate changes that can reduce your carbon footprint and save energy.

2. **Research Sustainable Materials**: Before your next electrical maintenance or upgrade, research the sustainable materials discussed and ask potential contractors about eco-friendly alternatives they could offer. From wiring to fixtures, every

little bit counts.

3. **Seek Out Eco-conscious Contractors:** When looking to hire electrical contractors, prioritise those who demonstrate a commitment to sustainability. Check their policies for energy efficiency, waste management, and whether they use sustainable materials.

4. **Discuss Durability and Maintenance:** Choose solutions that are not only sustainable but also durable. Longer-lasting materials may be more cost-effective over time, despite a higher upfront cost. Discuss maintenance plans with your contractor to ensure your electrical systems are operating efficiently.

5. **Evaluate the Impact on Property Value:** If you're considering major upgrades, think about how these could affect your property's value. Energy-efficient, sustainable homes can attract a premium in the real estate market.

6. **Promote and Participate in Green Initiatives:** Whether it's through your business or personal community, advocate for and participate in initiatives that promote sustainability. Sharing your journey and learning from others can amplify the impact of your actions.

Taking these steps not only contributes to a healthier planet but also aligns with a growing global trend towards sustainability that can be both personally and financially rewarding. Remember, every small change contributes to a larger impact, making each decision towards eco-friendly solutions a powerful step forward.

THE PSYCHOLOGICAL BENEFITS OF SIMPLIFIED CHOICES

"Too many choices can confuse us, simplicity liberates us." -
Barry Schwartz

Minimising Decision Fatigue

In today's world, where choices abound for just about everything from coffee flavours to whom you hire to fix your leaking tap, decision fatigue can quietly seep into your day-to-day life. This invisible drain on your mental batteries can affect not only your efficiency but also your ability to make sound decisions. Let's unpack what this means for you, especially when you're faced with selecting contractors or services for your home or business needs.

Understanding Decision Fatigue

Decision fatigue refers to the deteriorating quality of decisions made by an individual after a long session of decision making. It's like running a marathon but with your brain. The more choices you are forced to make, the more exhausted your brain becomes, leading to potentially poor decisions.

Imagine you are renovating your kitchen. You start your day choosing the design, then move on to the materials, followed by fixtures, and still, you need to decide on the contractor. Each choice uses up a slice of your mental energy. By the time you get to the last few decisions, you might just pick an option to finish the process, not because it's the best one.

This is particularly pertinent when you're bombarded with multiple quotes and proposals. It sounds diligent to gather numerous quotes, but each additional option requires more of your time to evaluate and adds to the cognitive load. You need to keep track of various details and differences - a fertile ground for decision fatigue to flourish.

How Fewer Choices Lead to Better Decisions

There's a sweet spot in decision-making: enough choices to feel in control, but not so many that you're overwhelmed. When you limit the number of quotes for a service to, say, three, you strike a balance between variety and manageability. This approach harnesses the paradox of choice where having too many options can lead to anxiety and indecision.

Reducing the number of choices helps in focusing more on quality rather than quantity. This focus allows you to thoroughly evaluate the available options based on their merits rather than rushing through each to simply get the process over with. When choices are manageable, you're more likely to consider all relevant factors, leading to a more informed and, ultimately, better decision.

Think about when you're in a restaurant with a five-page menu. The plethora of options often makes it difficult to choose, and you might end up either sticking to what you know or choosing something in haste. Now, imagine a menu with just a handful of carefully curated dishes. The decision is easier, and you might even try something new, confident that each option is crafted to please.

Strategies to Reduce Overload

To harness the full potential of simplified choices and combat decision fatigue, consider implementing these strategies:

1. **Prioritise Your Decisions**: Start your decision-making process by tackling the most important choices first when your mental energy is highest. For instance, if you're renovating, decide on the structural changes before the colours of the walls.

2. **Limit Your Options**: As discussed, keep your options limited. Whether it's quotes for a job or choices of paint colour, narrowing down your options to a manageable number can drastically cut down the mental clutter.

3. **Create a Decision-Making Framework**: Establish criteria for decision-making in advance. What are the must-haves and deal-breakers? This framework helps you quickly eliminate unfit options and makes comparing the remaining choices easier. For example, if hiring a contractor, essential criteria might include licensing, insurance, and previous work quality.

4. **Take Scheduled Breaks**: If you're making several decisions at once, take short breaks between them. This helps reset your mental state and reduces the carry-over effect of one decision on another.

5. **Leverage Technology**: Use apps and tools designed to compare options objectively. Many platforms can filter and sort choices based on your predetermined criteria, reducing the effort you need to put in.

6. **Trust Your Gut**: Sometimes, after you've used logical filters, trusting your instinct can be the tiebreaker. If one option feels particularly right, it might just be.

By simplifying the decision-making process, you not only make it easier to choose but also increase the likelihood of being satisfied with your decision. This approach doesn't just save time—it enhances the quality of your decisions, ensuring that you select the best contractor for the job without burning out your decision-making capacity. Remember, every decision counts, but not every decision should cost you peace of mind.

Confidence in Decision-Making

Building confidence with informed choices

Building confidence with informed choices starts with understanding that knowledge is power—especially when it comes to making decisions that impact your home or business. When you're faced with getting quotes for a service, the traditional advice has often been to get at least three to compare. However, in the pursuit of making the best choice, more quotes don't always mean better decisions; it often just leads to more confusion.

By limiting yourself to a single, well-researched quote, you streamline the process significantly. Start by doing thorough research on a single provider. Look into their credentials, reviews, past work, and even delve into their company values and customer service ethos. This focused approach allows you to gather in-depth knowledge about one provider rather than superficial details about many. You become better informed about your options, which in turn builds your confidence. You're not just choosing the least bad option among many; you're actively choosing the best possible option available.

This approach also helps in understanding the full scope of what the service involves. With one provider, you can spend more time asking questions and getting to know the person or team who will be working on your project. This not only demystifies the process but also makes you feel more in control. The confidence comes from a clear understanding of what to expect, how much it will cost, and how it fits into your broader goals for your home or business.

The role of instinct in contractor selection

The role of instinct in contractor selection is often undervalued in traditional decision-making frameworks, yet it plays a crucial part. Your gut feeling is a synthesis of many quick calculations your brain makes based on past experiences, knowledge, and your personal value system. When you simplify your choices, you give more room for your instincts to play a part.

With fewer options, you're not overwhelmed by data and can tune in to how you feel about the decision. Do you feel comfortable with the contractor? Do they seem trustworthy? Do they understand your vision? When choices are too numerous, these questions can get lost in the noise of trying to compare multiple complex options. Trusting your gut can sometimes lead to faster and more satisfying decision-making.

However, relying on instinct doesn't mean disregarding logical considerations. It means integrating that gut feeling with the informed research you've conducted. When these elements align, the decision usually feels right both logically and instinctually, which enhances your confidence in the choice made.

Overcoming second-guessing

Overcoming second-guessing is another critical aspect of confident decision-making. Second-guessing often occurs when there are too many options on the table, or when you feel underinformed about the choices made. By simplifying the process and choosing one quote after thorough vetting, you significantly reduce the grounds for doubt.

Once the choice is made, it's important to commit fully. Doubt can be further mitigated by setting clear, measurable expectations with the contractor before the work begins. Define the scope of the work, the timeline, and the cost upfront. Regular communication throughout the process also helps maintain confidence in your decision, as it reassures you that everything is proceeding according to plan.

Another good strategy to counteract second-guessing is to keep a decision journal. After you make the decision, write down why you chose that contractor and what the deciding factors were. Should doubt creep in, you can refer back to this journal. Reminding yourself of the reasons for your choice can reaffirm your confidence and help quash any lingering uncertainties.

In essence, confidence in decision-making when selecting a contractor comes from a blend of thorough research, trusting your instincts, and committing to your choice without overloading yourself with options. By focusing on one potential hire rather than several, you not only streamline the process but also enhance your overall confidence in the decisions you make. This approach not only simplifies the selection process but also contributes to a more satisfying and successful project outcome.

Satisfaction and Peace of Mind

Enjoying the Renovations Process

Embarking on a renovation project, whether it's revamping your kitchen or expanding your business premises, should be an exhilarating journey, not a stress-inducing nightmare. The traditional approach of soliciting multiple quotes often paints a picture of due diligence and thoroughness. However, paring down your options to a single, trusted quote simplifies the start of your project tremendously, setting a positive tone from the outset.

You might wonder how one can genuinely enjoy the process when there are so many horror stories about renovations gone wrong. The key lies in the peace of mind that comes from having made a confident, well-informed choice from the get-go. When you select a contractor based on a deep understanding of your needs and a solid rapport, you sidestep the anxiety of second-guessing your decisions at every turn.

This approach allows you to focus more on the creative aspects of the renovation. You can channel your energy into choosing designs, materials, and fixtures that resonate with your vision, rather than fretting over whether you've chosen the right person for the job. It's about trusting the process and enjoying the evolution of your space, secure in the knowledge that the project is in capable hands.

Feeling Secure in Your Choice

The foundation of feeling secure in your choice of contractor lies in your initial selection strategy. By opting for a single, thoroughly vetted quote rather than scattering your focus across multiple bids, you invest in a quality partnership from day one. This doesn't just minimise the risk of miscommunication—it builds a professional relationship based on clarity and mutual respect.

Security also stems from transparency. A contractor who provides a comprehensive, clear quote and who is willing to discuss and justify the cost provides a reassuring level of transparency that can often be diluted when dealing with multiple contractors. This transparency ensures that there are no surprises, fostering a sense of security that you are getting exactly what you paid for.

Moreover, this feeling of security is enhanced by the simplicity of having a single point of contact. There's a significant comfort in knowing that you have one dedicated professional who understands the full scope of your project and your expectations. This reduces the complexity and potential for errors that can occur when messages are filtered through multiple channels, which is often the case when dealing with several contractors.

Long-term Contentment with Results

The true measure of success in any renovation or building project is your contentment with the results long after the work has been completed. Single Quote Success isn't just about the immediate benefits of reducing choice overload; it's also about the long-term satisfaction that comes from excellent, consistent results.

Contentment arises when expectations are met or exceeded, and this is far more likely when you have developed a relationship with a single contractor who is fully attuned to your vision and standards. When a contractor fully understands your objectives and has been part of the planning process from the beginning, they are better positioned to deliver results that align with your expectations.

Furthermore, the assurance of quality workmanship carries forward years after the project is completed. Knowing that every aspect of the job was handled by a professional you trust means that you can look back on the decision without regrets, confident in the knowledge that it was the right choice. This long-term contentness is not just about the aesthetics of the finished work, but also about the enduring functionality and value added to your property.

Choosing to simplify the selection process by committing to one detailed, thoughtful quote can transform your renovation experience from a source of stress to a source of joy. It enables a relationship with a contractor that's based on mutual respect and understanding, leading to a smoother process and results that you can be proud of for years to come. The journey towards a successful renovation project is paved with many decisions, but by focusing on quality and trust from the outset, you ensure that the path leads to lasting satisfaction and peace of mind.

RECAP AND ACTION ITEMS

Congratulations on navigating through the rich insights around the psychological benefits of simplified choices! By now, you understand that reducing the number of quotes to consider does not just save time—it can significantly improve the quality of your decisions, boost your confidence, and enhance your overall satisfaction with the outcomes.

Let's boil down the essentials and set forth some actionable steps that you can implement immediately:

1. **Combat Decision Fatigue**: Remember, every decision you make, no matter how small, depletes your mental energy. To keep your decision-making capacity fresh and effective, limit yourself to evaluating no more than three quotes for any service or product you need. This approach not only streamlines your decision-making process but also preserves your energy for other critical tasks throughout your day.

2. **Strengthen Confidence in Your Choices**: Trust is key. When choosing a contractor or a service, go beyond the surface. Pick options that not only fit your budget and timeline but also align with your instincts about the provider's credibility and the quality of their past work. This trust, built on both facts and

intuition, will help you feel more confident in your decisions.

3. **Secure Peace of Mind**: With fewer options, you're less likely to second-guess yourself and more likely to enjoy the progress and results of your project. Once you've made a decision, commit fully and resist the urge to keep looking at other available options. This commitment will help you focus on managing the project effectively, leading to better outcomes and greater satisfaction.

Action Steps:

Next time you need to hire a service or buy a product, deliberately restrict the number of quotes you fetch.

Invest time in doing some preliminary research about each option. Check reviews, ask for referrals, and verify credentials before you even ask for a quote

Listen to your gut. If something feels off about a particularly low or high quote, take a step back and evaluate why

Once you've made a decision, throw your full support behind it. Communicate clearly and regularly with your chosen contractor to ensure all expectations are met.

By integrating these principles, you're not just making smarter choices—you're also setting yourself up for a smoother, more enjoyable experience in managing projects and making purchases. Here's to making life a little easier, one decision at a time!

MASTERING THE SINGLE QUOTE APPROACH

"Quality is more important than quantity. One home run is much better than two doubles." – Steve Jobs

Lessons Learned and Best Practices

Key Takeaways

So, you've decided to go against the grain and embrace the single quote approach—congratulations! This strategic shift can streamline your decision-making process, cut through the noise of endless options, and focus on quality and value. What have we learned from adopting this simplified strategy? Here are the key takeaways that you should embed in your toolkit:

1. **Efficiency Overload**: By soliciting just one quote, you minimise the time spent on vetting multiple contractors, thus speeding up the project initiation phase. This efficiency does not just save you time; it also reduces the cognitive load of comparing numerous variables, allowing you to make decisions

with clarity and confidence.

2. **Quality Connections**: When you opt for a single quote, it often means you are choosing a provider based on trust and previous positive outcomes. This singular focus enhances the quality of your interaction with the service provider, fostering a deeper, more meaningful connection.

3. **Cost Transparency**: One might assume that more quotes mean more competitive pricing. However, a single quote approach can lead to clearer cost structures. Given the mutual respect and understanding, providers are more likely to present their best, most honest price upfront, eliminating any hidden costs that sometimes arise with competitive bidding.

4. **Focus on Value**: This approach shifts the emphasis from price to value. You're encouraged to consider not just the cost but also the expertise and added benefits the contractor brings to your project. This perspective helps in choosing a contractor who aligns with your project's needs and goals.

Best Practices

Adopting the single quote approach might seem straightforward, but it requires a nuanced understanding of best practices to ensure success. Here's how you can optimise this strategy:

1. **Choose Wisely**: The foundation of the single quote method lies in selecting the right contractor. Do your homework—look for recommendations, check reviews, and verify credentials.

Choosing a contractor with a solid track record of reliability and excellence is paramount.

2. **Define Your Project Clearly**: Before you approach a contractor, have a clear idea of what your project entails. Detailed requirements can help the contractor provide an accurate and comprehensive quote. This clarity prevents misunderstandings and scope creep, thereby saving time and money.

3. **Negotiate Thoughtfully**: While the single quote approach simplifies selection, negotiation remains a critical element. Be open about your budget constraints and project expectations. A good contractor will help find a middle ground without compromising the quality of the outcome.

4. **Establish Clear Communication Channels**: Regular communication can make or break a project. Set up predefined times for updates and insist on transparent communication from the start. This practice helps in addressing issues promptly and keeping the project on track.

5. **Document Everything**: From the initial quote to the final agreement, ensure all discussions and agreements are well-documented. This not only provides a reference point but also protects both parties in case of disputes.

Tips and Advice for Future Homeowners

As a future homeowner or someone looking to dive into a new project, embracing the single quote approach can seem daunting. Here are some tailored tips to guide you:

1. **Educate Yourself**: Understand the basics of the service or construction process you are engaging in. A well-informed client can make more strategic decisions and communicate effectively with service providers.

2. **Seek Referrals**: Leverage your network to find trusted contractors. Personal referrals often lead to more reliable and personalised service experiences.

3. **Prioritise Compatibility**: Beyond skills and experience, choose a contractor who shares your communication style and project vision. Compatibility can significantly enhance the working relationship.

4. **Be Realistic**: Set realistic expectations about timelines and budgets. Discuss these aspects with your contractor to ensure there is mutual understanding and agreement.

5. **Plan for Contingencies**: Always have a backup plan. While the single quote approach focuses on a primary contractor, having a contingency plan ensures you're prepared for any unforeseen circumstances.

By integrating these lessons learned, best practices, and tips into your approach, you are more likely to experience a smoother, more successful project execution. Remember, the goal is not just to complete a project but to do so with less stress and more satisfaction. Embracing the single quote approach can significantly contribute to achieving this outcome, ensuring you not only meet but exceed your expectations.

Building Strong Contractor Relationships

Establishing Trust and Transparency

In the realm of home improvement or business renovation, the cornerstone of any successful project lies in the foundation of trust and transparency you build with your contractor. Think of it as constructing a metaphorical bridge between your vision and their execution. Commencing this journey with a single quote strategy, where you select one contractor to handle your entire project, amplifies the importance of establishing a solid, transparent relationship from the get-go.

Trust begins with open communication. It's essential to articulate your expectations clearly and listen attentively to the contractor's input. Remember, while you know what you want, contractors know how to get there. They can offer insights into the practical aspects of your project, suggest alternatives, and highlight potential pitfalls. By fostering a dialogue that accommodates both perspectives, you create a collaborative atmosphere where ideas can be exchanged freely and respectfully.

Transparency, on the other hand, involves a clear understanding of the project scope, timeline, budget, and the responsibilities of all involved parties. Ensure that your contractor provides a detailed proposal that outlines all aspects of the project. This document should not only break down costs but also timeline milestones and the materials to be used. Moreover, it should be dynamic enough to accommodate necessary adjustments along the way. Regular updates and honest feedback from your contractor can prevent misunderstandings and build a stronger relationship, ensuring that no one is left in the dark.

Leveraging Expertise and Innovation

Once trust is established and communication lines are open, leveraging your contractor's expertise and innovation becomes your strategic advantage. After all, you've chosen them for a reason, and their unique skills can bring a level of sophistication and efficiency to your project that might not be achievable otherwise.

Encourage your contractor to think creatively and to suggest innovative solutions that might not be immediately obvious. Whether it's the latest energy-efficient technology, a unique design layout, or a cost-effective material alternative, their input can often lead to better outcomes than originally anticipated. Remember, the goal is to enhance the project, not just get it done.

Moreover, in a world where technology evolves rapidly, staying abreast of the latest advancements in construction and project management tools can be incredibly beneficial. Many contractors now use sophisticated software to manage projects, keep track of budgets, and maintain timelines. Discuss these tools with your contractor and understand how they can be used to enhance your project's execution. This not only helps in keeping your project on track but also in making informed decisions quickly and efficiently.

Conflict Resolution Strategies

Even in the most well-planned projects, conflicts can arise. These might stem from unexpected project challenges, delays, or differences in vision. However, the approach to resolving these conflicts can make or break the relationship you have with your contractor.

Firstly, it's crucial to approach conflict with a problem-solving mindset, rather than a combative one. When an issue arises, discuss it directly with your contractor at the earliest opportunity. Avoid blame and instead focus on understanding the problem and exploring solutions together. Often, a compromise can be reached that satisfies both parties and may even bring an unexpected improvement to the project.

Secondly, establish a formal yet flexible process for handling disputes. This could involve regular check-ins where both parties can air concerns in a structured manner. Sometimes, bringing in a third-party mediator can offer a neutral perspective and help resolve deeper conflicts. Remember, the objective here is to preserve the relationship and keep the project moving forward, not just to win an argument.

Lastly, learn from each conflict. Reflect on what went wrong and why, and how similar situations can be avoided in the future. This not only helps in refining your approach to dealing with future issues but also strengthens the bond with your contractor, as they see your commitment to continuous improvement and mutual respect.

By embracing these strategies within the single-quote framework, you not only streamline the process but also create a partnership that is built to last. This approach not only brings your vision to life effectively but does so in a way that maximizes both satisfaction and success.

Achieving Long-Term Success

In the realm of managing projects and handling renovations or new builds, the end of a project isn't the end of the road. Rather, it marks a transition into a crucial phase where the true calibre of decisions made during the project starts to manifest. Here, we delve into how you can evaluate project outcomes effectively, sustain productive relationships beyond each project, and nimbly adapt to market changes, ensuring your long-term success.

Evaluating Project Outcomes

Once the dust has settled and the contractors have packed up, it's time to step back and assess the fruits of your labours. Evaluating project outcomes goes beyond just admiring the aesthetic upgrades or enjoying the new space. It involves a thorough analysis of the project against your initial objectives and expectations.

Start with the functionality of the completed work. Does everything work as intended? Are there any issues that weren't apparent during the final walkthrough? Sometimes, problems surface after living with the new changes for a few weeks. Make a list of any discrepancies and determine if they require immediate attention or if they can be scheduled for future maintenance.

Next, reflect on the financial aspect of the project. Did you stay within budget? If not, understand where the overruns occurred. Was it due to unforeseen circumstances, or perhaps a change in scope? Analysing these elements will help you manage future projects more effectively, preventing similar budget issues.

Also, consider the timeline of the project. Delays can be frustrating and costly. Were the timelines reasonable and adhered to, or did the project extend far beyond the expected completion date? Understanding the causes of delays can provide insights into how to better schedule future endeavours or whether to adjust your expectations about project durations.

Lastly, take into account your overall satisfaction with the project. This subjective measure is crucial. After all, the space is yours to live or work in. If there's something that isn't quite right, even if it's as minor as the finish on a fixture, note it down. This will be invaluable when planning future projects or recommending services to peers.

Sustaining Relationships Beyond the Project

Building and maintaining strong relationships with contractors and service providers can reap benefits that go beyond any single project. These relationships can lead to quicker response times for maintenance issues, potential discounts on future projects, and valuable advice when considering new ventures.

To keep these relationships flourishing, communication is key. Don't let the conversation end at the project's completion. A simple check-in email or a call can keep you at the forefront of their minds, making it easier to pick up where you left off when the next project arises.

Another way to sustain a good relationship is by providing feedback. Most service providers appreciate knowing what they did well and where they could improve. Constructive feedback is a tool that helps them refine their practice, and they'll likely be grateful for the honesty, which fosters loyalty and trust.

Additionally, don't underestimate the power of saying thank you. A gesture as simple as sending a thank you card, leaving a positive review online, or even a referral can go a long way in cementing a lasting professional relationship. Such acts show appreciation and respect for the work they've done, which is often reciprocated in their willingness to go above and beyond for you in the future.

Adapting to Market Changes

The market is continually evolving, influenced by new technologies, changing consumer demands, and economic shifts. Staying adaptable ensures not only the sustainability of your property but also its enhancement in value over time.

Keep abreast of new developments in construction and design by subscribing to relevant publications, attending workshops, and networking with industry professionals. This knowledge allows you to make informed decisions about upgrades or changes that could benefit your property in the long run.

Consider also the environmental impact of your choices. Sustainability isn't just a buzzword; it's a practical consideration that can affect property value and utility costs. Upgrading to energy-efficient windows or investing in renewable energy sources, for example, can significantly reduce bills and increase the appeal of your property in an environmentally-conscious market.

Lastly, be proactive rather than reactive. Regularly evaluate the state of your property and the market conditions. Is it a good time to sell? Should you renovate to increase value? By staying one step ahead, you can maximise your investments and maintain a strong position in the market, regardless of its fluctuations.

By taking these steps, you position yourself not just as a successful project overseer but as a savvy investor in your property's future. Each project completed is a stepping stone towards greater achievements, ensuring that every decision made is a building block to your long-term success.

RECAP AND ACTION ITEMS

You've now explored the intricate layers of the Single Quote Success method. By focusing on key takeaways, best practices, and invaluable tips, you've equipped yourself with a robust framework to enhance your decision-making process. This isn't just about simplifying; it's about empowering you with the confidence to choose wisely and foster relationships that last.

So, what's next? It's about putting this knowledge into action. Here are some practical steps to start implementing these insights immediately:

1. **Review and Reflect**: Take a moment to reflect on past experiences where you've sought multiple quotes. Consider the time, energy, and resources you used compared to the outcomes achieved. How might these situations have benefitted from the Single Quote approach?

2. **Identify Your Trusted Contractor**: Start by identifying a contractor or service provider who demonstrates transparency,

innovation, and trustworthiness. Initiate conversations to gauge their expertise and willingness to commit to the transparency you require.

3. **Set Clear Expectations**: When you approach your chosen contractor with a project, clearly outline your expectations regarding timelines, costs, and communication. This clarity will foster mutual respect and minimise potential conflicts.

4. **Build the Relationship**: Invest time in building a relationship beyond the immediate project. Regular check-ins and feedback sessions can help establish a long-term partnership that might benefit future projects.

5. **Stay Informed**: The market will continue to evolve, so keep yourself informed about new trends and technologies that could impact your decisions. This knowledge will not only improve your projects but also foster discussions with your contractor about innovative approaches.

6. **Evaluate and Adapt**: After completing a project, take the time to evaluate the outcomes against your initial expectations. Discuss what worked and what didn't with your contractor, and use these insights to refine your approach for next time.

By adopting the Single Quote approach, you're not just simplifying a process; you're strategically positioning yourself to achieve better outcomes, build stronger relationships, and enjoy greater peace of mind. Start small, perhaps with a minor project, and as you grow more comfortable, expand this approach to more significant ventures. Remember, success in this streamlined approach hinges not just on whom you choose, but on how you work together towards common goals.

SEIZE THE DAY: YOUR PATHWAY TO MASTERING CONTRACTOR CHOICE STRATEGIES

As our journey through contracting strategies comes to a close, it's crucial to reflect on the transformative concepts we've explored together. This book has been meticulously crafted to help homeowners navigate the complexities of contractor selection, empowering you to make informed decisions with confidence.

In today's homeowner landscape, understanding contract management isn't just advantageous—it's essential. Each chapter has equipped you with the knowledge and tools to not only comprehend but excel in selecting the right contractor with clarity and certainty. We've debunked myths, streamlined processes for efficiency, and fortified your ability to ensure quality outcomes—all crucial components of mastering the art of contractor selection.

Now, envision applying this newfound knowledge in practical scenarios. Picture the heightened effectiveness, the enhanced clarity, and the significant reduction in stress achievable when focusing on finding the right contractor from the start. These strategies aren't merely theoretical; they're actionable and transformative, poised to simplify your decision-making and ensure peace of mind throughout your home improvement projects.

Navigating through contractor options, assessing their expertise, and managing risks should now appear less daunting and more like a straightforward pathway ahead. These insights aren't just chapters in a book; they're pivotal chapters in your journey as a homeowner, contributing to a solid framework for achieving successful home improvements.

As you move forward, remember: the homeowner's landscape evolves constantly. Stagnation isn't an option for those striving to make the best choices for their homes. Continuous learning and adaptation are your allies. The insights and strategies shared here provide a solid foundation, but your approach will evolve based on your unique needs and experiences.

Take charge of your homeowner journey. Whether renovating, upgrading, or maintaining your home, these principles will serve as your guiding compass. Each decision, informed by these principles, propels you toward greater satisfaction and success with your home projects.

Nevertheless, the complexities of contractor selection sometimes demand specialized expertise. If you encounter challenges requiring tailored assistance, remember support is within reach. Don't hesitate to connect with professionals who can offer customized guidance. Visit www.pdelectrical.info to access expertise needed to navigate even the most complex home improvement decisions.

This isn't just the conclusion of a book; it's the commencement of your mastery in contractor selection. Each turned page has brought you closer to becoming a knowledgeable leader in managing your home improvement projects. Now is your time to shine, applying your newfound knowledge to achieve the excellence your home deserves.

About the Author

Paul Dunn is the owner and lead electrician at P. D. Electrical Services (SW) Limited, a reputable electrical service provider based in North Devon, UK. With a commitment to high-quality work and customer satisfaction, Paul and his team offer a wide range of services, including solar and battery storage solutions, electrical installations for holiday homes, consumer unit upgrades, EV car charger installations, rewires and alterations, and Electrical Installation Condition Reports (EICRs).

Paul is highly praised for his professionalism, promptness, and meticulous attention to detail. His clients appreciate the clear and fixed pricing, the comprehensive safety checks, and the high standard of work provided by P. D. Electrical. Many reviews highlight Paul's friendly and efficient service, noting that he often goes the extra mile to ensure customer satisfaction.

For more information about Paul Dunn and P. D. Electrical, visit pdelectrical.info.

You can connect with me on:
🌐 https://pdelectrical.info

Also by Paul Dunn

Paul Dunn, an experienced electrician and owner of P. D. Electrical, is also a prolific author who shares his expertise through various books. His works are aimed at homeowners, apprentices, and professionals in the electrical field, providing valuable insights and practical guidance.

Paul Dunn's expertise, both in practice and through his writing, makes him a trusted authority in the field of electrical services. His books are designed to empower readers with knowledge, whether they are undertaking home improvements, starting their careers, or seeking to improve their professional skills. For more information about Paul Dunn and his services, visit pdelectrical.info.

Reclaim the Power: Reclaim the Power: Capture the Sun, Control Your Energy, Conserve Your Wallet
Focusing on solar energy and sustainability, this book educates readers on how to harness solar power effectively. It covers the benefits of solar energy, how to implement solar solutions, and the financial advantages of controlling one's energy usage.

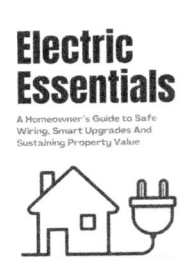

Electric Essentials: A Homeowner's Guide to Safe Wiring, Smart Upgrades, and Sustaining Property Value

A comprehensive guide for homeowners, this book addresses safe wiring practices, smart electrical upgrades, and ways to maintain and enhance property value. It serves as a practical manual for ensuring electrical safety and efficiency in the home.

Renovation Rethink: Scrutinising Proposals, Unveiling Expertise, and Achieving Desired Outcomes

This book guides homeowners through the renovation process, emphasizing how to critically evaluate proposals, leverage expert advice, and achieve desired results. It's an essential read for anyone looking to undertake a home renovation project.

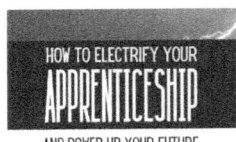

How to Electrify Your Apprenticeship: And Power Up Your Career

The first book in his Electrician's Success Path Series, aimed at apprentices and those starting in the electrical trade, this book provides career advice, practical skills, and insights into becoming a successful electrician. It covers everything from basic techniques to professional development strategies.

The Electrician's Blueprint: Navigate, Innovate & Thrive in Your Electrical Career

The second book in the Electrician's Success Path series, this book offers a roadmap for electricians seeking to advance their careers. It includes strategies for innovation, navigating the industry, and thriving as a professional electrician. It's a valuable resource for both new and experienced electricians.

Home Electric Mastery: Understand, Maintain, and Enhance Your House's Wiring

Unlock the secrets to safe and efficient home electrical systems with "Home Electric Mastery." This essential guide by Paul Dunn, a seasoned expert with over two decades of experience, demystifies the complexities of house wiring. From understanding basic principles to mastering advanced techniques, this book provides clear, practical advice for homeowners and budding electricians alike. Whether you're tackling minor repairs, planning upgrades, or ensuring compliance with regulations, "Home Electric Mastery" equips you with the knowledge and confidence to enhance your home's electrical safety and functionality.

Current Advances: Prepare Perfectly, Pass Professionally, Progress Positively

"Discover how to navigate the complexities of electrical inspections and assessments with confidence. Whether you're just starting out or looking to switch providers, this essential guide offers insider tips and a step-by-step compliance roadmap to ensure you pass inspections and thrive in the trade. Don't let outdated practices hold you back—equip yourself with the knowledge needed to excel in today's fast-paced industry

Printed in Great Britain
by Amazon